RELATIONAL DATABASE DESIGN

B/code

INFORMATION SYSTEMS SERIES

Consulting Editors

D. E. AVISON
BA, MSc, Phd, FBCS
Professor of Information Systems,
Department of Accounting and Management Science,
Southampton University,Southampton, UK.

G. FITZGERALD
BA, MSc, MBCS
Oxford Institute of Information Management
Templeton College, Oxford, UK

This series of student texts covers a wide variety of topics relating to information systems. It is designed to fulfil the needs of the growing number of courses on, and interest in, computing and information systems which do not focus on the purely technological aspects, but seek to relate these to business or organisational context.

Contents

6. Top-Down Data Analysis: The Fundamentals

7. Entity-Relationship Diagramming: Pragmatics

8. Data Dictionaries

9. Extensions to Entity-Relationship Diagramming

10. View Integration

11. Criminal Court Cases: A Case Study in Design

12. Physical Database Design: Volume and Usage Analysis

Foreword

The Blackwell Scientific Publications Series on Information Systems is a series of student texts covering a wide variety of topics relating to information systems. It is designed to fulfil the needs of the growing number of courses on, and interest in, computing and information systems which do not focus on the purely technological aspects, but seek to relate these to the business and organisational context.

The information systems area has been defined as the effective design, delivery, use and impact of information technology in organisations and society. Utilising this fairly wide definition, it is clear that the subject area is somewhat interdisciplinary. Thus the series seeks to integrate technological disciplines with management and other disciplines, for example, psychology and philosophy. It is felt that these areas do not have a natural home, they are rarely represented by single departments in polytechnics and universities, and to put such books into a purely computer science or management series restricts potential readership and the benefits that such texts can provide. This series on information systems now provides such a home.

The books will be mainly student texts, although certain topics may be dealt with at a deeper, more research-oriented level.

The series is expected to include the following areas, although this is not an exhaustive list: information systems development methodologies, office information systems, management information systems, decision support systems, information modelling and databases, systems theory, human aspects and the human-computer interface, application systems, technology strategy, planning and control, and expert systems, knowledge acquisition and representation.

A mention of the books so far published in the series gives a 'flavour' of the richness of the information systems world. *Information Systems Development: Methodologies, Techniques and Tools* (D.E. Avison and G. Fitzgerald), looks at many of the areas discussed above in overview form; *Information and Data Modelling* (D. Benyon), concerns itself with one very important aspect, the world of data, in some depth; *Structured Systems Analysis and Design Methods* (G. Cutts) looks at one particular information systems development methodology in detail; and *Multiview: An Exploration in Information Systems Development* (D.E. Avison and A.T. Wood-Harper) looks at an approach to information systems development which combines human and technical considerations; *Software Engineering for Information Systems* (D. McDermid) discusses software engineering in the context of information systems; *Information Systems Development: A Database Approach* (D.E.Avison) develops a database-oriented methodology for information systems development.

Paul Beynon-Davies' text on relational database design adds to the strength of the series on the data and database aspect. Whereas David Benyon's book concentrates on data modelling and David Avison's on a database approach to information systems development, this new text concentrates on relational databases. Whereas there are a number of texts containing a few chapters on relational databases, it is suprising that there are few solid texts looking solely at this subject, particularly as relational databases are now by far the most common database management systems on all types of computer. Paul Beynon-Davies has set out to provide a thorough and complete course on database design and he has achieved his objective admirably. There are lots of examples and case studies to integrate theory and practice and also a large number of diagrams to help further illustrate the concepts discussed.

The text also looks at a number of issues related to relational database management systems, often omitted from other texts, such as view integration, performance issues and a unique final chapter which examines the important sociological and semiological aspects. Paul Beynon-Davies' text represents an important contribution to the database literature and augments the strength of the Blackwell Scientific Publications Series on Information Systems in the database field.

David Avison and Guy Fitzgerald
Joint Consulting Editors
Information Systems Series

Preface

In the last twenty years or so the relational data model has stimulated a large amount of work in the area of database design. The results of this work have meant that database design has achieved far more of a formal footing. This change has made for some interesting developments in the way database design is taught.

In the past, for instance, courses concentrating solely on database design were the prerogative primarily of commercial training organisations. The emphasis in such courses was in providing 'rules of thumb' of good design practice usually directed at particular DBMS. Probably as a result of this emphasis, the average Polytechnic or University lecturer devoted a relatively small amount of time to this area, usually embedding the material in courses on database systems or systems analysis and design.

Contemporary opinion suggests that this is no longer a satisfactory state of affairs. The wealth of important material in this area has meant that nowadays, courses in database design (of at least two semesters length) are offered in most Polytechinics and Universities. Such courses usually build upon a foundation module in relational database systems.

Unfortunately, the literature on the subject has not kept apace with this change of emphasis. One still tends to see the computing literature site the subject primarily in textbooks on databases and/or systems development. What is needed are books addressed specifically to database design in general and relational database design in particular.

Whereas the companion volume, *Relational Database Systems*, in the Information Systems series discussed the general architecture of relational systems, the present work provides a pragmatic discussion of relational database design. It provides a considered and rounded introduction to the vast amount of material now written on the subject. In particular, the following themes run throughout the work:

(1) Most of the discussion in the text is centred around the application of a set of graphic techniques for the analysis and design of database systems. This is, of course, not unusual in itself. Most contemporary systems analysis and design techniques are heavily graphical in nature. What is different about the techniques discussed in this book

is that they form an integrated set. Hence, we shall show how a top-down technique like entity-relationship diagramming bears a close relationship to a bottom-up technique such as determinancy diagramming.

(2) Data analysis is a modelling skill. It is a task in abstraction. Much of what is called data analysis cannot therefore be taught in a simple step-by-step way. It has to be learned through tackling lots and lots of problems. To this end, many example problems with solutions are provided throughout the text to illustrate the concepts discussed. At the end of each chapter a set of exercises is provided which the reader is strongly advised to attempt. Sample solutions are provided at the back of the book. Appendix 1 provides a series of open-ended exercises for further practice.

(3) The techniques discussed cannot be properly understood without the context of a complete problem in application development. To this end, two levels of case study are provided throughout the text. Each chapter uses a small case study designed to bed the ideas discussed in a practical context. Chapter 11 describes a larger case study which uses most of the material discussed in the previous chapters in the development of a particular application.

(4) Computer-aided tools for database design work have blossomed over the last few years. Many such tools are now converging with some of the newer developments in computing such as hypermedia systems and artificial intelligence. To give the reader some understanding of this convergence we discuss in the conclusive chapter a system under development by the author and a number of colleagues at the Polytechnic of Wales.

(5) One of the main aims of the work is to highlight the distinction between relational database design in theory and relational database design in practice. The theory has tended to emphasise the value of formalism and various notations for database design. This is a limited conception of database design. The practical design of a database system is far more resonant with the interpretation of meaning - the shaping of reality.

I would like to thank a number of persons who have helped in the production of this work and its companion volume *Relational Database Systems*. Particular thanks to Prof. David Avison for carefully commenting on early drafts, Robin Arnfield for handling my proposals with exemplary speed and Janet Prescott for carefully proofing the works.

Chapter 1
Introduction

1.1 Introduction

In this chapter our aim is to highlight some of the key landmarks on the map which documents the terrain of database design. We define the concept of a database and data model, and distinguish between the relational data model and so-called semantic data models. This leads us to a discussion of the process of database design and the core stages in the design process. Then we consider how modern CASE (or CAISE) tools are being increasingly imbued with particles of 'intelligence'. Finally, we pinpoint some of the key problems in understanding and practising database design and highlight how a sociological and semiotic framework can help us in this practice.

1.2 Databases

A database is an organised repository for data. The overall purpose of such a system is to maintain data for some set of enterprise objectives. Normally, such objectives fall within the domain of administration. Most database systems are built to store the data required for the running of the day-to-day activities of some organisation.

The term organisation usually implies some hierarchical division. Hence we normally speak of a database as being a collection of files. A collection of files containing information on company employees, for instance, would normally constitute a database. Each file in a database is in turn also a structured collection of data. Each file is made up in turn of a series of records. These might be items of information, for instance, on each employee in a company.

Each employee record is divided up into a series of areas known as fields. Within each field a specific value is written. Occasionally we may wish to retrieve information about a given employee quickly. For this purpose we maintain an index which might store, for instance, the names of employees arranged in alphabetical order together with a reference to the physical location of the record for a given employee.

We shall encounter these terms again and again throughout this work. One of the major advantages of the relational approach to data is that it closely emulates this traditional physical organisation of data.

But what organisational purpose does a database serve? A database can be viewed as a model of reality. The information stored in a database is usually an attempt to represent the properties of some objects in the real world. Hence, for instance, a personnel database is meant to record relevant details of people. We say relevant, because no database can store all the properties of real-world objects. A database is therefore an abstraction of the real world. We shall return to this important issue of abstraction in chapter 9.

The question of organisation is therefore of fundamental importance to a database system. In database terms organisation further implies a series of properties:

(1) Data Sharing. Data held in a database is not usually there solely for the use of one person. A database is normally accessible by more than one person perhaps at the same time.

(2) Data Integration. This implies that a database should be a collection of data which has no unnecessarily duplicated or redundant data.

(3) Data Integrity. The database must accurately reflect the universe of discourse it is attempting to model. This means that the database should be subject to a series of business rules or integrity constraints.

(4) Data Security. One of the major ways of ensuring the integrity of a database is by restricting access, in other words, securing the database. The major way this is done in contemporary database systems is by defining in some detail a set of authorised users of the whole, or more usually parts of the database.

(5) Data Abstraction. Much emphasis has been placed on the database concept in recent years as a conceptual modelling tool. The major theme underlying database work is the attempt to model the logical structure of data and separate this from any physical implementation concerns.

(6) Data Independence. One immediate consequence of abstraction is the idea of buffering data from the processes that use such data. The ideal is to achieve a situation where data organisation is transparent to the users or application programs which feed off data.

1.3 Data Models: Architectures for Data

The term data model, like many other terms in computing, is somewhat ambiguous. In the literature the term is used in at least two senses. In the first sense, the term data model is used to describe an architecture for data. In the second sense, the term data model is used to describe the rules of some business application.

It is useful to make a direct analogy with building. The architecture of building is made up of some set of principles involved in determining how a building can be built from a set of component materials to some predetermined style. An architecture of building is made up of a set of components and techniques.

An architecture of data is similar in conception. The component materials are more abstract than the bricks and mortar of an architecture of building, but an architect of data still has to have some conception of how to build a database from underlying data structures.

In the second sense, the term data model is analagous to a completed building or perhaps more accurately to the design for a building. In an architectural design, the building architect will have applied some principles of architecture to satisfy the demands or requirements of his client. In a database design, the data architect will have modelled the rules of some enterprise, the requirements of his client, by applying the concepts of his data architecture.

1.4 Relational Data Model

Any data model, in the architectural sense, is generally held to be made up of three components (Tsitchizris and Lochovsky, 1982):

(1) A set of data structures.
(2) A set of data operators.
(3) A set of inherent integrity rules.

These three components are frequently referred to as data definition, data manipulation and data integrity respectively.

The relational data model is intrinsically simple. This is its primary appeal. As the American Architect Mies Van Der Rohe once said *'Less is More'*. There is only one data structure in the relational data model - the disciplined table or relation. The operators of the model all act on such tables to produce new tables. The operators are bundled together in a set known as the relational algebra. There are also only two inherent integrity rules in the relational data model. One is known as entity integrity, the other is called referential integrity.

To summarise, the relational data model is made up of one data structure, eight fundamental operators and two inherent integrity rules. To this we add a concern with controlling access to a database via the concept of a view.

1.5 Semantic Data Models

Data models are undoubtedly central to information systems work in two senses. First, they provide the conceptual basis for thinking about applications of a data-intensive nature. Second, they provide a formal basis for the tools and techniques of information systems building.

Brodie has made a distinction between three generations of data model (Brodie, 1984).

Primitive Data Models. In this approach objects are represented by record-structures grouped in file-structures. The main operations available are read and write operations over records. Third generation languages such as COBOL, at least in terms of a minimal definition of COBOL, primarily use primitive data models.

Classic Data Models. These are the hierarchical, network and relational data models. The hierarchical data model is a an extension of the primitive data model discussed above. The network is an extension of the hierarchical approach. The relational data model is a fundamental departure from the hierarchical and network approaches.

Semantic Data Models. The main problem with the classic data models is that they still maintain a fundamental record-orientation (McLeod and King, 1985). In other words, the meaning of the information in the database - its semantics - is not readily apparent from the database itself. Semantic information must be consciously applied by the user of databases using the classic approach. For this reason, a number of so-called semantic data models have been proposed. Semantic data models attempt to provide a more expressive way of representing the meaning of information than is available in the classic models.

1.6 Entity-Relationship Data Model

Probably the most frequently cited of the semantic data models is the entity-relationship data model (E-R model). The E-R Model was originally advocated by P.P.S. Chen (Chen, 1976). Intended to be a direct alternative to the relational data model it is now more commonly used as a conceptual modelling tool for database design. In this sense, the E-R model is now more clearly seen as an ally rather than an enemy of the relational data model.

In the E-R model the real world is represented in terms of entities, the relationships between entities and the attributes associated with entities. Entities represent objects of interest in the real world such as *employees*, *departments* and *projects*. Relationships represent named associations between entities. A department *employs* many employees. An employee *is assigned to* a number of projects. *Employs* and *is assigned to* are both relationships in the entity-relationship approach. Attributes are properties of an entity or relationship. *Name* is an attribute of the *employee* entity. *Duration of employment* is an attribute of the *employs* relationship.

The original entity-relationship model has been extended in a number of ways (Teorey et al, 1986). One of the most important extensions is the support for generalisation hierarchies (Smith and Smith, 1977). This allows us to declare certain entities as instances of other entities. For instance, *manager*, *secretary* and *technician* might all be declared instances of an *employee* entity. Likewise, *sales managers*, *production managers* etc. would all be declared instances of the *manager* entity. The important consequence of this facility is that entities lower down in the generalisation hierarchy inherit the attributes of entities higher up in the hierarchy. Hence, a *sales manager* would inherit properties of managers in general, and indeed of employees in general.

1.7 Schemas

A distinction is frequently made between the intension of a database and the extension of a database. These terms, taken from formal logic, describe the following aspects of a database:

(1) The intension of a database is a set of definitions which describe the structure of a given database. i.e., what data structures are used and what integrity constraints hold.

(2) The extension of a database is the total set of all data in a database.

Both the intension and extension of a database must conform to the tenets of a given data model. The intension of a database is frequently referred to as its schema. Hence, people frequently refer to a relational schema or an entity-relationship schema. We shall tend to reserve the word to refer to a design for a relational database.

1.8 What is Database Design?

Database design is a process of modelling. It is a process of successive refinement through three levels of model: conceptual models, logical models and physical models. A conceptual model is a model of the real world expressed in terms of entities, relationships, and attributes. A logical model is a model of the real world expressed in terms of relations, domains, primary keys and foreign keys. A physical model is a model of the real world expressed in terms of files and access structures such as indexes. Figure 1.1 summarises the process of database design.

Most conceptual models are built using constructs from the semantic data models. We shall use the extended entity-relationship model to

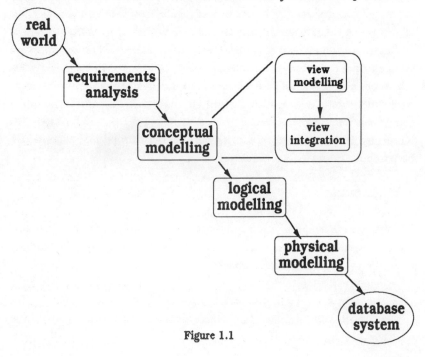

Figure 1.1

illustrate the process of building conceptual models. Most logical models are nowadays expressed using the constructs of the relational data model. In chapter 2 we shall outline the key concepts of the relational data model. Most existing relational database management systems are built around a core standard known as SQL (Structured Query Language). In chapters 12 and 13 we shall illustrate how to translate a logical model expressed as relations into a fine-tuned SQL database.

1.9 Stages of Database Design

There are hence three core stages to any database design task: conceptual modelling, logical modelling and physical modelling.

Some people see conceptual modelling as a stage headed by a require-ments analysis stage (e.g., Avison, 1991). The process of requirements analysis involves eliciting the initial set of information and processing requirements from users. The conceptual modelling stage can be thought of as comprising two sub stages: view modelling, which transforms the user requirements into a number of individual user views, and view integration which combines these views into a single *global schema* (Vossen 1990). The process of logical modelling is concerned with deter-mining the contents of a database independently of the exigencies of a particular physical implementation. This is achieved by taking the con-ceptual model as input, and transforming it into the data model support-ing the target database management system (DBMS). This is usually the relational data model. Physical modelling involves the transformation of the logical model into a definition of the physical model suitable for a specific software/hardware configuration. This is usually some schema expressed in the data definition language of SQL. Figure 1.1 illustrates these stages of database design.

Most existing database design techniques have been created for, or adapted to, the relational data model. The most prominent of such techniques are normalisation and entity-relationship modelling. Normali-sation is a technique based upon the work of Codd (Codd,1970). Some-times referred to as a *bottom-up* design technique, normalisation involves the transformation of data subject to a range of file-maintenance problems into a form free from such problems. Entity-relationship modelling is sometimes known as a *top-down* design technique, Entity-relationship modelling involves representing some universe of discourse in terms of entities and relationships. Both normalisation and E-R modelling have reached a certain degree of formalisation, and therefore would appear to be prime candidates for automation.

1.10 Intelligent CAISE for Database Design

Contemporary computer aided information systems engineering (CAISE) tools attempt to increase the productivity of system designers and programmers in a number of ways (Martin, 1984). For instance, contemporary database design tools provide graphical interfaces (such as E-R diagrammers), cross checking and validation of systems, and automation of much of the task of system documentation. Although such tools provide assistance in carrying out many design tasks with improved efficiency, they are largely the results of the automation of well established structured design techniques. Existing CAISE technology does not address the fundamental characteristic of design. Design is a knowledge-intensive activity that begins with an informal set of frequently vague requirements and ends up in a systematically defined formal object. Database design is therefore currently a labour-intensive process much prone to error. Also, the end-result of design is devoid of the design knowledge that led to its construction. It is precisely this design knowledge that is needed to maintain existing systems and develop new systems.

Artificial intelligence techniques can be used to develop a new generation of CAISE tools capable of overcoming many of these problems. Knowledge-based Information Systems engineering is likely to replace contemporary data-based Information Systems engineering. The current crop of data-based tools such as data dictionaries will be supplanted by knowledge-based tools. A knowledgebase is a database supplemented with rules and an inference engine that applies the rules. Whereas a data-based tool can merely reason about the structure of a contemporary database system, a knowledge-based tool will be able to reason about the semantics of a database system (Lowry and Duran, 1989).

1.11 Conclusion

In this chapter we have painted brief outlines of the key landmarks which we shall discuss in the chapters that follow. In the next chapter we shall discuss the relational data model and its implementation in the database sub-language SQL. Chapter 3 provides a number of different perspectives on the analysis of data - the key activity in contemporary database design.

Chapters 4 and 5 discuss in some detail a bottom-up approach to data analysis, known conventionally as normalisation. This is followed by a detailed consideration of top-down data analysis as expressed in a technique known as entity-relationship diagramming (chapters 6 and 7).

The reason why we cover a logical modelling technique before a conceptual modelling technique is purely for pedagogical reasons. It is the experience of the author that a sound appreciation of entity-relationship diagramming can only be gained once a sufficient understanding of the goal of a normalised relational model is achieved.

Chapter 8, 9, 10 and 11 extend our discussion of design techniques. Chapter 8 is devoted to a contrasting technique for documenting entity models - data dictionaries. Chapter 9 contains a brief overview of the technique of view integration, while chapter 10 discusses some important extensions to entity-relationship diagramming. Chapter 11 details a case study in which we apply all of the material from the earlier chapters.

The concluding chapters of this work address the practical task of database design. Chapters 12 and 13 discuss the important topic of turning a logical model into a physical database design. Chapter 14 turns our attention to the growing range of tools for aiding database design. Chapter 15 sets database design in a sociological and semiotic framework.

1.12 Exercises

(1) Define the term database.
(2) Describe the main properties of a database system.
(3) Define the term database management system (DBMS).
(4) Define the term data model.
(5) Discuss the distinction between an architectural data model and a business data model.
(6) Why is the relational data model not usually regarded as being a semantic data model?
(7) In what way is database design a modelling exercise?
(8) Describe the main stages of database design.
(9) What is meant by the acronym CAISE?

Chapter 2
Relational Database Systems

2.1 Introduction

In this chapter we provide a brief overview of relational database systems. For a more detailed discussion of this topic the reader is referred to the companion volume to this work (Beynon-Davies, 1991b).

We begin our discussion with a definition of the component parts of the relational data model: data definition, data manipulation, and data integrity. We then consider each component in turn. The second half of the chapter provides a brief overview of what is emerging as the standard core of any relational DBMS - the database sub-language SQL.

2.2 Data Models

In chapter one we defined any data model, in the architectural sense, as being made up of three components:

(1) A set of data structures (data definition).
(2) A set of data operators (data manipulation).
(3) A set of inherent integrity rules (data integrity).

We now discuss each of these component parts in turn and highlight how they apply in the relational data model.

2.3 Data Definition

A database is effectively a set of data structures for organising and storing data. In any data model we must have a set of principles for exploiting such data structures for business applications. Data definition is the process of exploiting the inherent data structures of a data model for a particular business application.

One of the major attractions of the relational data model is its simplicity. It is simple because it has only one data structure - the disciplined table or relation. Although the structures below are tables in common parlance, to E.F.Codd, the creator of the relational data model, they are relations.

A relation is a table which obeys a certain restricted set of rules:

EMPLOYEES

Empno	Ename	Job	Mgr	Hiredate	Salary	Comm	Deptno
7369	Smith	Clerk	7902	17-DEC-80	800		20
7499	Allen	Salesman	7698	20-FEB-81	1600	300	30
7521	Ward	Salesman	7698	22-FEB-81	1250	300	30
7566	Jones	Manager	7839	02-APR-81	2975		20
7654	Martin	Salesman	7698	28-SEP-81	1250		30
7698	Blake	Manager	7839	01-MAY-81	2850		30
7782	Clarke	Manager	7839	09-JUN-81	2450		10
7788	Scott	Analyst	7566	09-NOV-81	3000		20
7839	King	President		17-NOV-81	5000		10
7844	Turner	Salesman	7698	08-SEP-81	1500	0	30
7876	Adams	Clerk	7788	23-SEP-81	1100		20
7900	James	Clerk	7698	03-DEC-81	950		30
7902	Ford	Analyst	7566	02-DEC-81	3000		20
7934	Miller	Clerk	7782	23-JAN-82	1300		10

DEPARTMENTS

Deptno	Dname	Location
10	Accounting	London
20	Research	Bristol
30	Sales	London
40	Operations	Birmingham

(1) Every relation in a database must have a distinct name.

(2) Every column in a relation must have a distinct name within the relation.

(3) All entries in a column must be of the same kind.

(4) The ordering of columns in a relation is not significant.

(5) Each row in a relation must be distinct. In other words, duplicate rows are not allowed in a relation.

(6) The ordering of rows is not significant. There should be no implied order in the storage of rows in a relation.

(7) Each cell or column/row intersection in a relation should contain only a so-called atomic value. In other words, multi-values are not allowed in a relation.

To enforce the property that duplicate rows are forbidden each relation must have a so-called *primary key*. A primary key is one or more columns of a table whose values are used to uniquely identify each of the rows in a table.

Primary keys are of fundamental importance to the relational data model. This is because, in combination with the table or relation name, a primary key value provides the sole addressing mechanism in the relational data model. In other words, the only guaranteed way of locating a given row from a relational database is via a combination of table name and primary key value. This is the reason that the relational data model is often referred to as a value-oriented data model (Ullman, 1989).

The primary unit of data in the relational data model is the data item, for example, a part number, a customer number or a person's date of birth. Such data items are said to be non-decomposable or atomic. A set of such data items of the same type is said to be a *domain*. For example, the domain of customer numbers is the set of all possible customer numbers. Domains are therefore pools of values from which actual values appearing in the columns of a table are drawn.

According to Codd, the concept of a domain has played a very important role in the development of the relational data model. One reason for this is that if two columns draw their values from the same domain then comparisons between these columns make sense. Hence a comparison between the *deptno* column of the *employees* table and the *deptno* column in the *departments* table has some validity. In contrast, a comparison between employee names and department names does not make sense. We may have an employee with the surname *London*, but people are different objects from departments. They draw their values from different domains.

Foreign keys are the 'glue' of relational systems. They are the means of interconnecting the information stored in a series of disparate tables. A foreign key is a column or group of columns of some table which draws its values from the same domain as the primary key of some other table in the database. In our personnel example *deptno* is a foreign key in the *employees* table. This column draws its values from the same domain as the *deptno* column - the primary key- of the *departments* table. This means that when we know the *deptno* of some employee we can cross-refer to the *departments* table to see, for instance, where that employee is located.

2.4 Data Manipulation

Data manipulation has four aspects:

(1) How we input data into a relation.
(2) How we remove data from a relation.

(3) How we amend data in a relation.

(4) How we retrieve data from a relation.

When Codd first proposed the relational data model by far the most attention was devoted to the final aspect of data manipulation - information retrieval. That is, how we run queries on our database and extract information to satisfy these queries. It is only relatively recently in his publications on version 2 of the data model that Codd has devoted considerable attention to the other three conventional aspects of data manipulation (Codd, 1990).

In his early papers, Codd proposed a collection of operators for manipulating relations (Codd, 1970). He called the entire collection of such operators the relational algebra. Codd's intention was to demonstrate a theoretical retrieval language which operated on entire relations and produced relations as results (see figure 2.1).

The relational algebra is a set of some eight operators. Each operator takes one or more relations as input and produces one relation as output. The three main operators of the algebra are *select*, *project* and *join*. Using these three operators most of the manipulation required of relational systems can be accomplished. The additional operators - *product*, *union*, *intersection*, *difference* and *division* - are modelled on the traditional operators of set theory.

Relational Algebra = Manipulative Part Of Relational Model

ALGEBRAIC OPERATORS ACT ON WHOLE RELATIONS

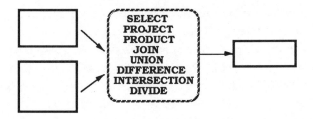

Figure 2.1

(1) Select/Restrict. The *select* or *restrict* operator of the relational algebra takes a single relation as input and produces a single relation as output. Select is a 'horizontal slicer'. It extracts rows from the input relation matching a given condition and passes them to the output relation.

(2) Project. The *project* operator takes a single relation as input and produces a single relation as output. *Project* is a 'vertical slicer'.

(3) Product. The relational operator *product* is a direct analogue of a set-theoretic operation known as the *Cartesian Product*. A *product* takes two relations as input and produces as output one relation composed of all the possible combinations of input tuples.

(4) Join. The *join* operator takes two relations as input and produces one relation as output. A number of distinct types of *join* have been identified. Probably the most commonly used is the *natural join*, a development of the *equi-join*.. The *equi-join* operator is a *product* with an associated *select*. In other words, we combine two tables together but only for records matching a given condition. Natural join is an equi-join followed by a project of one of the join columns.

(5) Union. *Union* is an operator which takes two relations having the same structure as input and produces one relation as output. The output relation is composed of all the rows of the two input relations.

(6) Intersection. Whereas *union* produces the combination of two sets or tables, *intersection* produces a result table which contains rows common to both input tables.

(7) Difference. Using *difference*, the order of specifying the input tables matters. Difference table 1 table 2 gives us all tuples in table 1 not in table 2. Difference table 2 table 1 gives us all tuples in table 2 not in table 1.

(8) Division. *Divide* takes two tables as input and produces one table as output. One of the input tables must be a binary table, i.e., it must have two columns. The other input table must be a unary table, i.e., a one column table. The unary table must also be defined on the same domain as one of the columns of the binary table. The fundamental idea of *divide* is that we take the values of the unary table and check them off against the compatible column from the binary table. Whenever all values from the unary table match with the same value from the binary table, we output the value to the result table.

2.5 Data Integrity

When we say a person has integrity we normally mean we can trust what that person says. We assume, for instance, a close correspondence between what that person says and what he or she does.

When we say a database has integrity we mean much the same thing. We have some trust in what the database tells us. There is a close correspondence between the facts stored in the database and the real world it models. Hence, in terms of our personnel database we believe that the fact - *Scott is a member of the Research Department* - is an accurate reflection of the workings of our enterprise.

It is useful to make a distinction between inherent and additional integrity. Inherent integrity is built into the data model itself. A database to be truly relational for instance must satisfy the two inherent integrity rules of the relational data model - *entity* and *referential integrity*. Additional integrity is non-inherent. Additional integrity must be specified by means other than the data model.

Entity integrity concerns primary keys. Entity integrity is an integrity rule which states that every table must have a primary key and that the column or columns chosen to be the primary key should be unique and not null.

Referential integrity concerns foreign keys. The referential integrity rule states that any foreign key value can be in one of two states. The usual state of affairs is that the foreign key value refers to a primary key value of some table in the database. Occasionally, and this will depend on the rules of the organisation, a foreign key value can be null. In this case we are explicitly saying that either there is no relationship between the objects represented in the database or that this relationship is unknown.

2.6 The Database Sub-language SQL

One of the major formalisms which define the present generation of relational database management products is Structured Query Language or SQL for short. SQL was originally designed as a query language based on the relational algebra. SQL however is a lot more than simply a query language - Codd refers to it as a database sub-language.This database sub-language is becoming the standard interface to relational and non-relational DBMS.

SQL comes in 3 major parts:

(1) A data definition language (DDL) with integrity enhancement.

(2) A data manipulation language (DML).

(3) A data control language (DCL).

2.6.1 Data Definition Language

Suppose that we have a company requirement to produce a database of information. The structure for each of the tables in the database can be set up using the create table command. For example:

```
CREATE TABLE SALES
(sales_no char(4),
product_no char(4),
customer_no char(4),
qty number(3))
```

The create table statement allows us to specify a name for a table, and the names, data-types and lengths of each of the attributes in the table. Many contemporary implementations of SQL have no direct mechanism for enforcing the notion of primary and foreign keys. An addendum to the ANSI standard (ANSI, 1989) however specifies a primary and foreign key clause:

```
CREATE TABLE SALES
(sales_no char(4),
product_no char(4),
customer_no char(4),
qty number(3))
PRIMARY KEY (sales_no)
FOREIGN KEY (customer_no IDENTIFIES customers)
FOREIGN KEY (product_no IDENTIFIES products)
```

Referential integrity also involves specifying precisely what should happen in related tables when updates and deletes occur in a target table. The specifications below restrict the deletion of a department record until all matching employee records have been deleted. They also specify that any change made to the department number of a department's record should be reflected in all relevant employee records.

```
CREATE TABLE departments
(deptno NUMBER(2),
dname CHAR(10),
loc CHAR(10))
PRIMARY KEY (deptno)

CREATE TABLE employees
(empno NUMBER(4),
ename CHAR(10),
job CHAR(9),
mgr NUMBER(4),
hiredate DATE,
salary NUMBER(7,2),
comm NUMBER(7,2),
deptno NUMBER(2))
PRIMARY KEY (empno)
FOREIGN KEY (deptno identifies departments,
DELETE OF deptno RESTRICTED,
UPDATE OF deptno CASCADES)
```

When a table is created information is written to a number of system tables. This is a meta-database which stores information about the structure of tables at the base level. Information about a table or an index can be removed from the system tables by using the DROP command:

```
DROP TABLE sales
```

Only a certain amount of amendment activity is allowed on table structures by SQL. We can add an extra attribute to a table:

```
ALTER TABLE employees
ADD (age num(3))
```

We can also modify the size of an existing attribute:

```
ALTER TABLE employees
MODIFY (job char(20))
```

2.6.2 Data Manipulation Language

Having created a structure for the tables in our database, we can enter data into such tables using the INSERT command:

    INSERT INTO Customers
    (customer_no,name,area)
    VALUES
    (01,'Friendly Foods','Cardiff')

If the list of values is in the same sequence as the sequence of attributes in the table, the sequence of attribute names can be omitted:

    INSERT INTO Customers
    VALUES
    (01,'Friendly Foods','Cardiff')

We also maintain the ongoing data in the database through use of the update and delete comands:

    UPDATE Customers
    SET Sales_area = 'Valleys'
    WHERE Customer_no = '01'

    DELETE FROM Customers
    WHERE Customer_no = '01'

Although SQL has a data definition and file maintenance subset, the language was designed primarily as a means for extracting data from a database. Such extraction is accomplished through use of the *select* command: a combination of the *restrict, project*, and *join* operators of the relational algebra.

Simple retrieval is accomplished by a combination of the *select, from* and *where* clauses:

    SELECT employee_no, name, job
    FROM employees
    WHERE job = 'Programmer'

The list of attribute names can be substituted with the wildcard character '*', in which case all the attributes in the table are listed:

```
SELECT *
FROM employees
WHERE job = 'Programmer'
```

To produce a sorted list as output we add the order by clause to the select statement:

```
SELECT employee_no, name, job, salary
FROM employees
WHERE job = 'Programmer'
ORDER BY salary
```

The default order is ASCII ascending. To produce the list in descending order we add the keyword DESC.

```
SELECT employee_no, name, job, salary
FROM employees
WHERE job = 'Programmer'
ORDER BY salary DESC
```

To undertake aggregate work such as computing the average salary of employees in a particular department we use the GROUP BY clause:

```
SELECT deptno, avg(sal), count(*)
FROM employees
WHERE deptno IN (10,20)
GROUP BY deptno
```

Note the use of the IN operator to specify a range of matchable values.

The *structure* in Structured Query Language originally referred to the ability to nest queries in select statements. For instance, to find out who makes more money than Jones we would write:

```
SELECT employee_no, name
FROM employees
WHERE salary >
(SELECT salary
FROM employees
WHERE name = 'Jones')
```

SQL evaluates the innermost query first. This produces a result which is compared with the result produced from the outermost query.

SQL performs relational joins by indicating common attributes in the where clause of a *select* statement. For instance, the *select* statement below extracts data from the salesforce and customers tables of relevance to salesmen working in the Valleys sales area, and orders it by the salesman_no attribute.

```
SELECT salesman_no, salesman_name, customer_no,
customer_name
FROM salesforce, customers
WHERE salesforce.sales_area = customers.sales_area
AND customers.sales_area = 'Valleys'
ORDER BY salesman_no
```

2.6.3 Data Control Language

The primary mechanism for enforcing control issues in SQL is through the concept of a view. Views are virtual tables which act as 'windows' on the database of real tables. The view below establishes a virtual table for use by salesmen working in the Valleys sales area. Salesmen granted access only to this view would be unable to see information of relevance to other sales areas in the company's sales profile.

```
CREATE VIEW VALLEYS
AS SELECT Customer_no, Customer_name, Sales_no, Product_no,
Qty
FROM Sales, Customers
WHERE Sales.Customer_no = Customers.Customer_no
AND Sales_area = 'Valleys'
```

This view defines limited access for users on all customers in the valleys area. The view becomes a table definition in the system catalog and remains unaffected by changes in the underlying sales and customers table.

Access can be restricted on tables and views to particular users via the *grant* and *revoke* facilities of SQL. *Grant* allows users read and file maintenance privileges on tables or views. *Revoke* takes such privileges away.

GRANT SELECT ON sales TO pbd

GRANT INSERT,UPDATE
ON customers
TO pbd

REVOKE SELECT,INSERT
ON customers

2.7 Conclusion

The relational data model has been unusual in that it was originally proposed as an abstract machine. Codds' intention was to build a formal model of data storage and manipulation independent of how data would be stored and processed on given hardware by given software.

The level of abstraction associated with the relational data model encouraged not only developments in database sub-languages such as SQL. It also encouraged the use of abstraction in considering what it means to capture the requirements of some application and design a database that conforms to the tenets of the relational data model. It is to this topic of data analysis that we now turn.

2.8 Exercises

(1) What was Codd's intention in creating the relational data model?
(2) Define the three parts of a data model.
(3) What makes a relation distinct from a table?
(4) Distinguish between a primary and foreign key.
(5) Define the operation of the three most important primitives of the relational algebra: restrict, project and join.

(6) Why is SQL defined as being a database sub-language?

(7) How does an SQL select differ from a relational algebra select?

(8) Define the two inherent integrity rules of the relational data model.

(9) What is meant by a view in SQL?

(10) Why is the system catalog so important for relational systems?

Chapter 3
Data Analysis

3.1 Introduction

In this chapter we discuss the central process of contemporary database design, a process frequently referred to as data analysis or data modelling. We first examine a number of perspectives on this activity which gives us a clearer idea of the overall objectives of data analysis. We then portray a number of distinct ways in which to conduct data analysis. Each of these approaches will be discussed in some depth in further chapters.

3.2 Data Analysis as Modelling

In chapter 1 we discussed two meanings for the term data model. This is a term used to refer either to an architecture for data or to a model of the workings of some enterprise or part of some enterprise. Data analysis concerns itself with both interpretations of the term data model. Data analysis is the process of building a business data model and representing it as a relational schema.

In this sense, data analysis takes a number of data models under its wing. For instance, we shall use one data model, namely the entity-relationship data model to help us conduct the process of conceptual modelling. We shall use another data model, the relational data model, to represent our logical database schema.

3.3 Data Analysis as Diagramming

Most of the techniques used in contemporary systems analysis and design are graphical in nature. Diagrams are held to be better communication tools than conventional narrative text. They are, for instance:

(1) Easier to produce.
(2) Easier to understand.
(3) Much more concise.
(4) Are better able to express 2-dimensional inter-connection.
(5) Rough versions of diagrams are easily made and re-drafted.

In chapters 4 to 8 we shall introduce two major diagramming notations: entity-relationship diagramming and determinancy diagramming. When our database designs get large however we shall find that many of the advantages listed above no longer hold true. In such situations a more tractable solution is provided for documenting design decisions in the shape of a data dictionary.

3.4 Data Analysis as User and Peer Group Participation

All stages of data analysis should be subject to some form of user and peer group review. This is particularly important at the requirements analysis stage. User involvement has been shown to produce better systems in terms of a closer match between user requirements and delivered systems. Peer group review of the products of design via techniques such as structured walkthroughs (Beynon-Davies, 1989) has been shown to reduce the number of errors in systems (Yourdon, 1978).

It is interesting that many of the techniques we shall be discussing in this work, such as entity-relationship diagramming, are conventionally portrayed solely as design tools. We shall also emphasise the important role they have to play as communication tools, particularly in the capture of requirements.

3.5 Data Analysis and Information Engineering

Originated in the work of Finklestein and Martin (Martin, 1984), information engineering has been an effective complement to software engineering. Information engineering is defined by Martin in the following terms:

> *The term software engineering refers to the set of disciplines used for specifying, designing and programming computer software. The term information engineering refers to the set of interrelated disciplines which are needed to build a computerised enterprise based on data systems. The primary focus of information engineering is on the data that are stored and maintained by computers and the information that is distilled from these data* (Martin, 1984).

Martin discusses the way in which information engineering builds itself on a number of premises:

(1) That data lie at the centre of modern data processing.

(2) That the types of, or structure of, data used in an organisation do not change very much.

(3) That given a collection of data, we can find a way to represent it logically.

(4) That although data are relatively stable, the processes that use this data change rapidly.

(5) That because data remain relatively stable, whereas processes are subject to rapid change, data-oriented techniques succeed if correctly applied where process-oriented techniques have failed.

Figure 3.1 illustrates the basic idea underlying these premises. The skyscraper blocks represent individual applications or processes which are subject to rapid change. All such processes are built on the same bedrock - information engineered foundations, which, by their very nature, must remain relatively stable.

3.6 Data Analysis and the Corporate Information Architecture

In recent years it has become clear that information is a resource of high

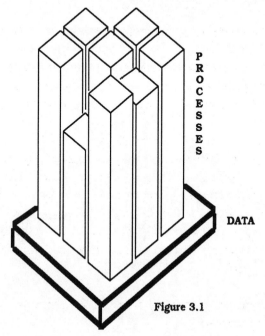

Figure 3.1

value to organisations. In this sense, data, viewed as a corporate asset, must be managed in the same way as any other corporate resource. In other words, information resource management pertains to data in the same way as human resource management pertains to people. Data, like people, are subject to sound management principles.

Information resource management has emerged as a discipline for managing not only the data needed to support the activities of an organisation, but also for planning the use of information for competitive advantage. The aim of information resource management is to develop a complete corporate information architecture. This architecture defines the structure of a company's data. It defines a data model for the entire enterprise.

Figure 3.2 illustrates the extending role of organisational data. No longer is it sufficient to see data merely as a means of handling the routine, administrative tasks of the organisation. Data can also be used in a more proactive role as a means of strategically improving the market share of a company. Earl (1989), for instance, cites numerous examples of the way in which data embodied in information technology can take on a more strategic and tactical role.

3.7 Data Analysis and CAISE

Database development is an information system in itself. As such, it is possible for it to be subject to, and benefit from, the same sorts of automation that characterise everyday information systems. This recur-

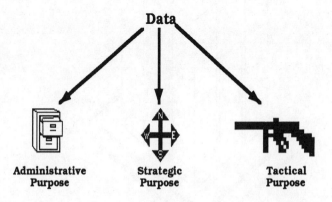

Figure 3.2

sive view of database development has been given a number of names. Perhaps the most popular is Computer Aided Software Engineering (CASE).

The term CASE however has a tendency to be associated with the process-oriented nature of software engineering. For this reason, the author prefers the acronym CAISE (Computer Aided Information Systems Engineering).

Backend CAISE has been particularly effective in the database arena. Around any contemporary relational DBMS, for instance, one will find a whole host of application building tools such as report generators, fourth generation languages, spreadsheets etc. Front-end CAISE has been equally effective in providing design tools such as graphics editors and data dictionaries. What is less well-established are the important links between front-end and back-end. Relatively few environments exist which provide a seamless join, for example, between a data model constructed with some appropriate editor and a generated application.

3.8 Data Analysis and Knowledge Engineering

Knowledge engineering is the discipline devoted to building knowledge base systems. As discussed elsewhere (Beynon-Davies, 1991a), the distinction between database systems and knowledge base systems is gradually fading. As database systems look for more functionality, the application of artificial intelligence appears more and more relevant.

As a consequence, what we conventionally know as data analysis today, we will probably refer to as knowledge analysis tomorrow. One particularly promising area seems to be the application of an object-oriented approach to the design of database systems. We discuss this topic in chapter 9.

3.9 Approaches to Data Analysis

There are normally held to be three complementary approaches to doing data analysis: top-down, bottom-up and laterally (more conventionally known as view integration).

Doing data analysis top-down means we use a diagramming technique such as entity-relationship diagramming to map what we believe to be the things of interest to the enterprise and the relationships between these things of interest. Top-down data analysis is frequently referred to as conceptual modelling because we remain at a high-level or on a fairly abstract plane. The product of such a modelling exercise is usually an entity-relationship diagram such as the one shown on figure 3.3. This diagram can be transformed into a set of table-structures - a relational schema - via a straightforward process of translation or accommodation.

Entity-relationship diagrams are also used in lateral data analysis. Here a series of differing viewpoints collected from various members of the organisation are plotted. These viewpoints are then integrated by super-imposing each upon the other and attempting to reach a state of compromise. The eventual model can be translated into a relational schema via a similar process as for top-down data analysis.

Rather than dealing with abstract concepts, bottom-up data analysis deals with concrete data. To do bottom-up data analysis we must have a pool of data items, extracted probably from an examination of existing enterprise documentation. To this pool of data items we apply a series of transformation rules. Bottom-up data analysis is also called normalisation.

3.10 Conclusion

In this chapter we have painted a number of perspectives of the data analysis exercise. Data analysis is the core of the database development

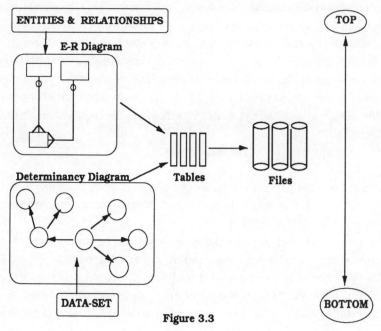

Figure 3.3

activity. It is a heavy user of graphic techniques founded in user and peer group participation. It has been used not only in the development of specific database projects, but also as a discipline for planning corporate information architectures. In its modern guise, data analysis is a heavy user of CAISE technology and is being greatly influenced by developments in the knowledge base systems area.

In the following chapters we start to add flesh to some of this discussion. We first look at bottom-up data analysis.

3.11 Exercises

(1) Define the term data analysis.

(2) Discuss modelling in the context of database development.

(3) Why are most contemporary database design techniques pictorial in nature?

(4) Why is user and peer group participation so important to data analysis?

(5) Define what is meant by the term information engineering.

(6) Why is data analysis important to corporate data planning?

(7) CAISE is incestuous: discuss.

(8) How is knowledge engineering important to data analysis?

(9) Discuss the distinction between top-down and bottom-up data analysis.

Chapter 4
Bottom-Up Data Analysis

4.1 Introduction

In his seminal paper on the relational data model, E.F. Codd formulated a number of design principles for a relational database (Codd, 1970). These principles were formalised in terms of three normal forms: first normal form, second normal form and third normal form. The process of transforming a design through these three normal forms is known as normalisation. By the mid-1970s third normal form was shown to have certain inadequacies and a stronger normal form, known as Boyce-Codd normal form was introduced (Codd, 1974). Subsequently Fagin introduced fourth normal form and indeed fifth normal form (Fagin 1977, 1979).

In this chapter we shall discuss all five normal forms. In particular, we shall consider their practical use as a design technique.

4.2 File Maintenance Anomalies

Suppose we are given the brief of designing a database to maintain information about patients and wards in a General Hospital. An analysis of the documentation presently used by the hospital gives us the following sample data set with which to work. If we pool all the data together in one table as below, a number of problems would arise in maintaining this data set.

Ward Name	Ward Type	No of Beds	Sister	Patient No.	Patient Name	Date of Birth
Bryn Siriol	Paediatric	6	N Hughes	3424	J Beynon	05-JAN-87
Bryn Siriol	Paediatric	6	N Hughes	2567	T Jones	10-MAR-88
Bryn Siriol	Paediatric	6	N Hughes	6789	R Burton	21-APR-89
Cefn Coed	Geriatric	8	T Evans	4545	F Davies	05-MAR-05
Cefn Coed	Geriatric	8	T Evans	3434	E Evans	10-OCT-10
Merthyr	General	10	M Thomas	2344	R Collier	10-JUN-67

(1) What if we wish to discharge patient *R Collier?* The result is that we lose some valuable information. We lose information about *Merthyr* ward. This is called a deletion side-effect.

(2) What if we transfer patient number *6789* into intensive care? We

need to update not only the ward type but also the name of the ward, its sister and the number of beds. This is called an update side-effect.

(3) What if we admit a new patient, say *7777, G Vaughn* to the *Ortho-paedics* ward? We need to know more information, namely about the *Orthopaedics* ward. This is an insertion side-effect.

(4) We change the position of the sister *N Hughes*. She transfers from *Paediatrics* to the *General* ward. We now have to update 3 different records in the file. This is an update side-effect again.

The size of our sample file is small. One can imagine the seriousness of the file-maintenance anomalies mentioned above multiplying as the size of the file grows. The above organisation is therefore clearly not a good one for the data of this enterprise. Normalisation is a formal process the aim of which is to reduce file maintenance anomalies.

4.3 Stages of Normalisation

Normalisation is carried out in the following steps:

(1) Represent the data as an unnormalised table.
(2) Transform the unnormalised table to first normal form.
(3) Transform first normal form tables to second normal form.
(4) Transform second normal form tables to third normal form.

Occasionally, the data may still be subject to anomalies in third normal form. In this case, we may have to perform further steps:

(5) Transform third normal form to fourth normal form.
(6) Transform fourth normal form to fifth normal form.

The process of transforming an unnormalised database into a fully normalised database is frequently referred to as a process of non-loss decomposition (see figure 4.1). This is because we continually fragment our data structure into more and more tables without losing the funda-mental relationships between data-items.

4.4 Representing the Data as an Unnormalised Table

Suppose we are given the task of designing a database for a major car

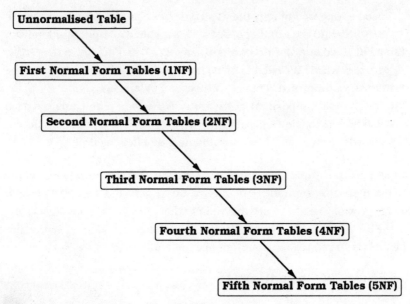

Figure 4.1

distributor. An analysis of this business leads us to suspect that the data-items illustrated in figure 4.2 are the most relevant to car distribution. Our first task is to build a sample data-set for this business in the form of an unnormalised table. This table is illustrated in figure 4.2.

Daley's Cars

Model	Style	Engine	Capacity	Max Speed	Price	Market	Main Competitor
macho	convertible	2900s	2847	155	12,900	sports	expresso
macho	coupe	2900s	2847	155	11,340	executive	gyro
macho	coupe	2400s	2395	131	9,950	executive	gyro
fiasco	saloon	2400s	2395	117	10,950	executive	gyro
fiasco	estate	2400s	2395	117	11,470	commuter	trio
fiasco	saloon	2400t	2395	101	9,990	executive	gyro
fiasco	estate	2400t	2395	101	10,370	commuter	trio
commando	saloon	2400t	2395	105	8,400	commuter	trio
commando	estate	2400t	2395	105	8,700	commuter	trio
commando	saloon	1900	1898	83	7,100	commuter	trio
domino	saloon	1900	1898	91	4,990	domestic	poncho
domino	estate	1900	1898	91	5,350	domestic	poncho
domino	saloon	1400	1365	79	4,450	domestic	poncho
domino	hatchback	1400	1365	79	4,100	domestic	poncho

Figure 4.2

Another way of viewing this structure is as a *universal relation*. The universal relation is a relation made up of all the attributes of a proposed database. The term *universal relation assumption* is used to describe the assumption that all the relations in a fully normalised database are derived from the universal relation by appropriate projection.

4.5 Unnormalised Table to First Normal Form

We transform an unnormalised table to first normal form by identifying repeating groups and turning such repeating groups into separate tables. We first choose a key for this data-set. Let us suppose we choose the data-item *model*.

Having chosen a key for the unnormalised table we look for a group of data-items that has multiple values for a single value of the key. Examining the table in figure 4.2 we see that every data-item repeats with respect to *model*. We therefore form a separate table of all the repeating data-items and transfer *model* across as a foreign key (see figure 4.3).

We continue this process by taking *model* and *style* to be the compound key of the table *bodies*. Here we see that *engine*, *capacity*, *max speed* and *price* all repeat with respect to this key. *Market* and *main competitor* do not.

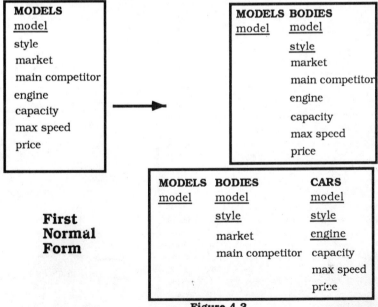

Figure 4.3

Splitting off the repeating attributes now gives us three tables which we have chosen to designate as *models*, *bodies* and *cars*. Note, the data-items *model*, *style* and *engine* now become the key of the new table. This decomposition gives us the tables in figure 4.4.

4.6 First Normal Form to Second Normal Form

To move from first normal form to second normal form we remove part-key dependencies. This involves examining those tables that have a compound key and for each non-key data-item in the table asking the question:

Can the data-item be uniquely identified by part of the compound key?

Take, for instance, the table named *cars*. Here we have a 3-part compound key. We ask the question above for the data-items *capacity, max speed* and *price*. Clearly we need all the values of *model*, *style* and *engine* to tell us what the price of a given car is going to be. *Style* however has no influence on the maximum speed of a car. Likewise, *model* and *style*, have no in-

MODELS

Model
macho
fiasco
commando
domino

CARS

Model	Style	Market	Main Competitor
macho	convertible	sports	expresso
macho	coupe	executive	gyro
fiasco	saloon	executive	gyro
fiasco	estate	commuter	trio
commando	saloon	commuter	trio
commando	estate	commuter	trio
domino	saloon	domestic	poncho
domino	estate	domestic	poncho
domino	hatchback	domestic	poncho

BODIES

Model	Style	Engine	Capacity	Max Speed	Price
macho	convertible	2900s	2847	155	12,900
macho	coupe	2900s	2847	155	11,340
macho	coupe	2400s	2395	131	9,950
fiasco	saloon	2400s	2395	117	10,950
fiasco	estate	2400s	2395	117	11,470
fiasco	saloon	2400t	2395	101	9,990
fiasco	estate	2400t	2395	101	10,370
commando	saloon	2400t	2395	105	8,400
commando	estate	2400t	2395	105	8,700
commando	saloon	1900	1898	83	7,100
domino	saloon	1900	1898	91	4,990
domino	estate	1900	1898	91	5,350
domino	saloon	1400	1365	79	4,450
domino	hatchback	1400	1365	79	4,100

Figure 4.4

fluence on a car's capacity, while *model* and *engine* is a key to *max speed*. This leads to a decomposition of the tables as in figures 4.5 and 4.6.

4.7 Second Normal Form to Third Normal Form

To move from second normal form to third normal form we remove inter-data dependencies. To do this we examine every table and ask of each pair of non-key data-items:

Is the value of field A dependent on the value of field B, or vice versa?

If the answer is yes we split off the relevant data-items into a separate table.

The only place where this is relevant to our present example is in the table called *bodies*. Here, *market* determines *main competitor*. Whenever we get a value for *market*, we unambiguously know what the *main competitor* is. We therefore create a separate table to be called *markets* with *market* as the key. This is illustrated in figure 4.7 and 4.8.

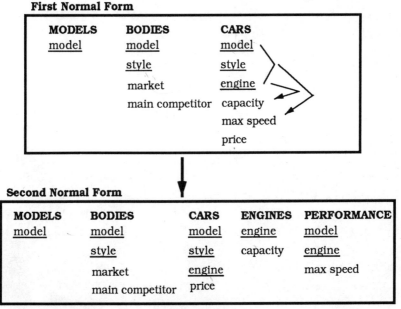

Figure 4.5

MODELS

Model
macho
fiasco
commando
domino

PERFORMANCE

Model	Engine	Max Speed
macho	2900s	155
macho	2400s	131
fiasco	2400s	117
fiasco	2400t	101
commando	2400t	105
commando	1900	83
domino	1900	91
domino	1400	79

ENGINES

Engine	Capacity
2900s	2847
2400s	2395
2400t	2395
1900	1898
1400	1365

CARS

Model	Style	Engine	Price
macho	convertible	2900s	12,900
macho	coupe	2900s	11,340
macho	coupe	2400s	9,950
fiasco	saloon	2400s	10,950
fiasco	estate	2400s	11,470
fiasco	saloon	2400t	9,990
fiasco	estate	2400t	10,370
commando	saloon	2400t	8,400
commando	estate	2400t	8,700
commando	saloon	1900	7,100
domino	saloon	1900	4,990
domino	estate	1900	5,350
domino	saloon	1400	4,450
domino	hatchback	1400	4,100

BODIES

Model	Style	Market	Main Competitor
macho	convertible	sports	expresso
macho	coupe	executive	gyro
fiasco	saloon	executive	gyro
fiasco	estate	commuter	trio
commando	saloon	commuter	trio
commando	estate	commuter	trio
domino	saloon	domestic	poncho
domino	estate	domestic	poncho
domino	hatchback	domestic	poncho

Figure 4.6

4.8 The Normalisation Oath

A useful mnemonic for remembering the rationale for normalisation is the distortion of the legal oath presented below:

(1) No Repeating,
(2) The Fields Depend Upon The Key,
(3) The Whole Key,
(4) And Nothing But The Key,
(5) So Help Me Codd.

Line 5 simply reminds us that the techniques were originally developed by E.F.Codd in the 1970s. Line 2 states that all data items in a table must depend solely upon the key. Line 1 indicates that there should be no repeating groups of data in a table. Line 3 indicates that there should be no part-key dependencies in a table. Finally, line 4 reminds us that there should be no inter-data dependencies in a table. The only dependency should be between the key and other data-items in a table.

Second Normal Form

MODELS	BODIES		CARS	ENGINES	PERFORMANCE
model	model		model	engine	model
	style		style	capacity	engine
	market ———————	→	engine		max speed
	main competitor ←		price		

↓

Third Normal Form

MODELS	MARKETS	CARS	ENGINES	PERFORMANCE
model	market	model	engine	model
	main competitor	style	capacity	engine
BODIES		engine		max speed
model		price		
style				
market				

Figure 4.7

4.9 De-Normalisation

Few data analysts would treat the file organisation proposed by third normal form as gospel. In real-life, the organisation proposed by third normal form usually represents too many files to be managed practically within the context of a given information system. Many sites would therefore regard first normal form to be good enough, particularly if data volumes are small, or transaction rates are low. Other sites may consider second normal form tables to be sufficiently flexible to meet the demands of higher volumes of data and transactions. Yet other sites may merge bits of third normal form relations together to optimise processing requirements. These issues will be discussed in more detail in chapter 13.

4.10 Fourth and Fifth Normal Forms

First normal form deals with repeating groups. Second and third normal forms deal with part-key and inter-data dependencies. Fourth and fifth normal forms deal with multi-valued dependencies. A multi-valued dependency is one in which one value of data-item A is associated with a delimited set of values for data-item B. Hence, for instance, a given employee number may have more than one dependent name associated

MODELS

Model
macho
fiasco
commando
domino

PERFORMANCE

Model	Engine	Max Speed
macho	2900s	155
macho	2400s	131
fiasco	2400s	117
fiasco	2400t	101
commando	2400t	105
commando	1900	83
domino	1900	91
domino	1400	79

CARS

Model	Style	Engine	Price
macho	convertible	2900s	12,900
macho	coupe	2900s	11,340
macho	coupe	2400s	9,950
fiasco	saloon	2400s	10,950
fiasco	estate	2400s	11,470
fiasco	saloon	2400t	9,990
fiasco	estate	2400t	10,370
commando	saloon	2400t	8,400
commando	estate	2400t	8,700
commando	saloon	1900	7,100
domino	saloon	1900	4,990
domino	estate	1900	5,350
domino	saloon	1400	4,450
domino	hatchback	1400	4,100

BODIES

Model	Style	Market	Main Competitor
macho	convertible	sports	expresso
macho	coupe	executive	gyro
fiasco	saloon	executive	gyro
fiasco	estate	commuter	trio
commando	saloon	commuter	trio
commando	estate	commuter	trio
domino	saloon	domestic	poncho
domino	estate	domestic	poncho
domino	hatchback	domestic	poncho

MARKETS

Market	Main Competitor
sports	expresso
executive	gyro
commuter	trio
domestic	poncho

ENGINES

Engine	Capacity
2900s	2847
2400s	2395
2400t	2395
1900	1898
1400	1365

Figure 4.8

with it. In a sense, fourth and fifth normal forms are also about compound keys. As we shall see, these normal forms attempt to minimise the number of data-items involved in a compound key.

4.11 Third to Fourth Normal Form

To move from third to fourth normal form we look for tables that contain two or more independent multi-valued dependencies. Multi-valued dependencies are fortunately scarcer than part-key or inter-data dependencies. Our car distributor problem therefore does not contain any such dependencies. We therefore examine here an example first discussed by Kent (1983).

Suppose we wish to design a personnel database for the Commission of the European community, which stores information about an employee's skills and the languages an employee speaks. An employee is likely to have several skills (e.g., typing, word-processor operation, spreadsheet operation), and most employees are required to speak at least two languages. We further add the restriction that each employee exercises skill and language use independently. In other words, typing as a skill is not inherently linked with the ability to speak a particular language.

Under fourth normal form these two relationships should not be represented in a single table as in figure 4.9. Instead, we split the table into two as in figure 4.10.

If we relax one of our constraints and now say that skill and languages are not independent then our structure changes somewhat. In other words, we are now saying we wish to record a person's ability to type in German. In this case the structure in figure 4.10 does not violate fourth normal form.

EMPLOYEES

Employee No.	Skill	Language
01	Typing	English
01	Word-Processing	English
01	Spreadsheet	English
01	Typing	French
01	Word-Processing	French
01	Spreadsheet	French
01	Typing	German
01	Word-Processing	German
01	Spreadsheet	German

Figure 4.9

4.12 Fourth Normal Form to Fifth Normal Form

Generally speaking, a fourth normal-form table is in fifth normal form if it cannot be non-loss decomposed into three or more smaller tables.

SKILLS		LANGUAGES	
Employee No.	Skill	Employee No.	Language
01	Typing	01	English
01	Word-Processing	01	French
01	Spreadsheet	01	German

Figure 4.10

OUTLETS

Agent	Company	Product
Jones	Ford	Car
Jones	Vauxhall	Van
Smith	Ford	Van
Smith	Vauxhall	Car

Figure 4.11

Consider the table in figure 4.11 which stores information about agents, automobile companies and automobiles. If agents represent companies, companies make products, and agents sell products, then we might want to record which agent sells which product for which company. To do this we need the structure in figure 4.12. We cannot decompose the structure because although agent Jones sells cars made by Ford and vans made by Vauxhall he does not sell Ford vans or Vauxhall cars.

If however another business rule becomes relevant. Namely that if an agent sells a certain product and he represents the company making that product, then he sells that product for the company. This means that we can now split up the information into three tables, and know that we can reconstitute the original information (see figure 4.13).

We know therefore that a table is in fifth normal form when its information content cannot be reconstructed from several smaller tables.

OUTLETS

Agent	Company	Product
Jones	Ford	Car
Jones	Ford	Van
Smith	Vauxhall	Van
Smith	Vauxhall	Car
Jones	Vauxhall	Car
Jones	Vauxhall	Van

Figure 4.12

AGENTS

Agent	Company
Jones	Ford
Smith	Vauxhall
Jones	Vauxhall

PRODUCTS   **COMPANIES**

Agent	Product	Company	Product
Jones	Car	Ford	Car
Jones	Van	Ford	Van
Smith	Van	Vauxhall	Van
Smith	Car	Vauxhall	Car

Figure 4.13

4.13 Conclusion

Classic normalisation is described as a process of non-loss decomposition. The decomposition approach starts with one (universal) relation. File maintenance anomalies such as insertion, deletion and update anomalies are gradually removed by a series of projections. Non-loss decomposition is therefore a design process guaranteed to produce a data-set free from file-maintenance problems. It does however suffer from a number of disadvantages, particularly as a practicable database design technique:

(1) It requires all of the data-set to be in place before the process can begin.
(2) For any reasonably large data-set the process is:
    (a) extremely time-consuming.
    (b) difficult to apply.
    (c) prone to human error.

The following chapter describes a contrasting approach to normalisation which uses a graphical notation. This makes the technique easier to use and less prone to error.

4.14 Exercises

(1) Define normalisation.

(2) What is meant by non-loss decomposition?

(3) What is the universal relation and what is the assumption associated with it?

(4) Define first normal form

(5) Define second normal form.

(6) Define third normal form.

(7) Define fourth normal form.

(8) Define fifth normal form.

(9) What is meant by de-normalisation?

(10) Produce third normal form table structures from the unnormalised relation below.

orders

order no.	order date	customer no.	customer name	product no.	product name	qty	unit price
0/23	01/02/91	2235	Davies	487	tiles (blue)	200	0.25
0/24	08/02/91	3444	Jones	488	tiles (white)	300	0.20
0/25	10/02/91	3444	Jones	489	tiles (red)	150	0.25
0/23	01/02/91	2235	Davies	340	grout (1kg)	10	1.25
0/24	08/02/91	3444	Jones	340	grout (1kg)	30	1.25
0/24	08/02/91	3444	Jones	342	cement (1kg)	30	1.50
0/26	01/02/91	2237	Evans	488	tiles (white)	400	0.20

Chapter 5
Determinancy Diagramming

5.1 Introduction

There are at least two approaches to normalisation. The traditional method, first espoused by Codd (Codd, 1970), and enhanced by numerous other researchers (Dutka and Hanson,1989), uses a step-by-step approach to database design. This decomposition approach, which was discussed in the previous chapter, has proven an excellent vehicle for explicating the intricacies of relational database design. It suffers as a practical design method however in that it is extremely difficult to apply to a large data set.

In this chapter we shall therefore discuss an alternative technique which exploits the advantages arising from the use of diagrams. The technique, known variously as determinancy diagramming or dependency diagramming, is a process of synthesis. This synthesis approach is a practical, two-step process for producing a good database design. In the first step, we build up, in an iterative manner, a diagram representing the relationships between data-items. In the second step, we take the completed diagram and apply a series of well-defined rules to arrive at a relational schema.

Both the decomposition and synthesis approaches described here are based upon a large amount of formal work. Those interested in this formal underpinning are referred to Dutka and Hanson, 1989.

5.2 Determinancy and Dependency

Normalisation is the process of identifying the logical associations between data-items and designing a database which will represent such associations but without suffering the file maintenance anomalies discussed in section 4.2. The logical associations between data-items that point the database designer in the direction of a good database design are referred to as determinant or dependent relationships. Two data-items, A and B, are said to be in a determinant or dependent relationship if certain values of data-item B always appear with certain values of data-item A.

Determinancy/dependency also implies some direction in the association. If data-item A is the determinant data-item and B the dependent data-item then the direction of the association is from A to B and not vice versa.

5.3 Functional and Non-Functional Dependency

There are two major types of determinancy or its opposite dependency: functional, (single-valued) determinancy, and non-functional (multi-valued) determinancy.

5.3.1 Functional (single-valued) Determinancy

Data-item B is said to be functionally dependent on data-item A if for every value of A there is one, unambiguous value for B. In such a relationship data-item A is referred to as the determinant data-item, while data-item B is referred to as the dependent data-item. Functional determinancy is so-called because it is modelled on the idea of a mathematical function. A function is a directed one-to-one mapping between the elements of one set and the elements of another set. Let us consider some examples of functional dependencies.

Example 1. In a personnel database, *employee_number* and *employee_name* are in a functional determinant relationship. *Employee_number* is the determinant and *employee_name* is the dependent data-item. This is because for every employee number there is only one associated value of employee name. For example, *7369* may be associated with the value *J.Smith*. This does not mean to say that we cannot have more than one employee named *J.Smith* in our organisation. It simply means that each *J.Smith* will have a different employee number. Hence, although there is a functional determinancy from employee number to employee name the same is not true in the opposite direction - employee name does not determine employee number.

Example 2. Staying with the table of employees information, employee number will probably functionally determine department number. For every employee there is only one associated department number which applies. An employee cannot belong to more than one department at any one time.

Example 3. In the table of departments information *department_number* is likely to functionally determine *location*. Every department is sited at just one location.

5.3.2 Non-Functional (multi-valued) Determinancy

Data-item B is said to be non-functionally dependent on data-item A if for every value of data-item A there is a delimited set of values for data-item B. The mapping is no longer functional because it is one to many.

Example 1. Consider adding an extra data-item to our personnel table - *employee skill*. Let us assume that our company maintains a large, coded list of human skills relevant to the company. The company wishes to record which employees have which skills. Clearly the relationship between employee numbers and skills is not a functional determinancy. Some employees may just have one skill, but most will have two or more skills.

Employee_number and *skill* are in a non-functional or multi-valued determinancy. In other words, for every *employee number* we can identify a delimited set of skill codes which apply to that employee.

Example 2. The same is true for the data-item *dependent name*. Many employees will have just one dependent but most will have two or more. *Employee_number* and *dependent_name* are members of a multi-valued or non-functional dependency.

Example 3. Finally, let us consider the case in which we wish to record, particularly for those working in the research department, the projects these employees are working on. The important point that this example emphasises is that determinant relationships are fundamentally business rules. One company may enforce the rule that an employee is assigned to only one project at any one time. Hence, in this company, the relationship between employee number and project number is a functional one. In another organisation the rule may be that an employee can be assigned to more than one project, but perhaps no more than three projects at one time. This makes the relationship between employee number and project number a multi-valued determinancy.

5.4 Notation

A diagram which documents the determinancy or dependency between data-items we shall refer to as a determinancy or dependency diagram. Data-items are drawn on a determinancy diagram as labelled ovals, circles or bubbles. Functional dependency is represented between two data-items by drawing a single-headed arrow from the determinant data-item to the dependent data-item. For example, figure 5.1 represents a number of functional relationships as determinancy diagrams.

Multi-valued or non-functional dependency is indicated by drawing a double-headed arrow from the determinant to the dependent data-item. Figure 5.2 represents two non-functional relationships as determinancy diagrams.

Dependencies between any two data-items may be diagrammed as A to B or B to A, but not both. Frequently, we may find that what is a functional dependency in one direction is a multi-valued dependency in the opposite direction. For example, take *employee_number* and *department_number*. In the direction *employee_number* to *department number* it is a functional dependency. In the direction *department_number* to *employee_number* it is a multi-valued dependency. In such situations we always choose the direction of the functional dependency. This makes the eventual relational

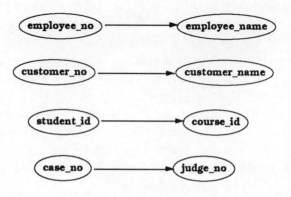

data-item B is functionally dependent on data-item A if for every value A there is only one distinct and associated value for B

Figure 5.1

**data-item B is non-functionally dependent
on data-item A if for any single value of A
there is an associated set of values for
data-item B**

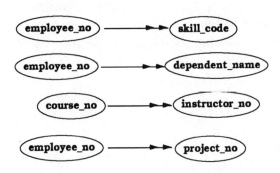

Figure 5.2

schema a lot simpler. It reduces, for instance, the number of compound keys required.

If however, a functional or non-functional dependency exists in both directions then we choose either. For example, *employee_number* might functionally determine *extension_number* and *extension_number* in turn functionally determines *employee_number*. We hence may choose either *employee_number* or *extension_number* as our determinant. Our choice is however likely to be influenced by how many other dependencies arise from the data-item. *Employee_number* is more likely to do more work for us in this context. More data-items are likely to be dependent upon *employee_number* than upon *extension_number*.

5.5 Transitive Dependency

Consider the following simple table.

Manager	Department	Location
Evans	Accounts	Cardiff
Jones	Marketing	Newport
Davies	Research	Swansea
Thomas	Production	Bridgend

By examination, we can identify three functional determinancies in this
table, one from *manager* to *department*, one from *department* to *location*,
and one from *manager* to *location*. What we have in this table is a transitive
determinancy. In other words, any situation in which A determines B, B
determines C and A also determines C can be simplified into the chain A
to B and B to C. Identifying transitive determinancies can frequently
simplify complex determinancy diagrams and indeed is an important part
of the process of normalisation. Figure 5.3 illustrates this process.

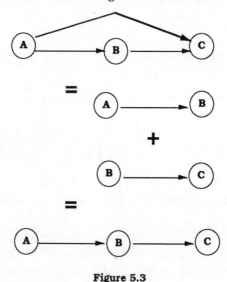

Figure 5.3

5.6 Compound Determinants

It is frequently found that one data-item is insufficient to fully determine
the values of some other data-item. The combination of two or more data-
items however gives us a dependent relationship. In such situations we
call the group of determinants a compound determinant. A compound
determinant is drawn as an enclosing bubble around two or more data-
item bubbles. Hence, in figure 5.4 we need both *order_no* and *product_no*
to functionally determine *qty*. The functional dependency is drawn from
the outermost bubble.

5.7 Accommodating Functional Dependencies

In this and the following section we examine the process of transforming
a determinancy diagram into a set of table structures or relational schema

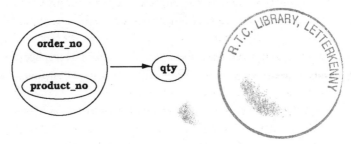

Figure 5.4

- a process frequently known as accommodation.

Suppose we are given the determinancy diagram in figure 5.5. We transform the diagram in figure 5.5 into a set of table structures by applying the rule:

Every functional determinant becomes the primary key of a table.
All immediate dependent data-items become non-key attributes
of the table.

This is frequently referred to as the Boyce-Codd rule after its inventors.

Figure 5.5

5.8 The Bracketing Notation

To represent the relational schema in an implementation-independent form we use a notation sometimes known as the bracketing notation. We list a suitable mnemonic name for the table first, This is followed by a list of data-items or column names delimited by commas. It is conventional to list the primary key for the table first and underline this data item. If the primary key is made up of two or more attributes, we underline all the component data items. For instance,

<relation name> (<u>primary key</u>, <column name>, ...)
customers(<u>customer no</u>, customer_name)

A number of other conventions are usefully applied to the bracketing notation:

(1) Table names are referenced by plural nouns, such as customers, employees, orders etc.
(2) Data-items or attributes are referenced by singular nouns such as employee_no, customer_no, order_no.
(3) If a data-item name is made up of two or more words then we use an underline character as a connector.

We can extend the basic bracketing notation with two useful devices for detailing the characteristics of foreign keys. If a foreign key can be null we enclose the data item name in curly brackets - { }. If the foreign key cannot be null we enclose the data item name in square brackets - [ ].

5.9 Drawing Boundaries

A useful intermediate step to take in the accommodation process is to draw boundaries around data-items of a determinancy diagram that form elements of table structures. The number of determinants (ovals with arrows emerging) should indicate the number of tables required. We have two determinants in figure 5.5, hence we need two tables. We also include within a boundary all the immediate dependent data-items (ovals with arrows converging). We hence draw two boundaries for our example as illustrated in figure 5.6. Note that foreign keys are easily identified on determinancy diagrams. They are usually ovals with arrows both emerging and converging. Deptno is a foreign key in figure 5.6.

Applying the functional and non-functional dependency rules to the diagram in figure 5.6 gives us the following table structures in the bracketing notation.

Employees(<u>employee-no</u>, employee_name, dept_no)
Departments(<u>dept-no</u>, location)

We then have to decide whether or not the foreign key *dept_no* should be allowed to be null or not. Let us suppose we decide it should be not null.

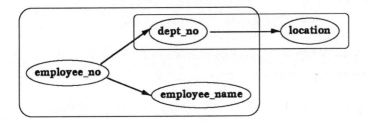

Figure 5.6

We annotate our schema as follows:

> employees(<u>employee no</u>, employee_name, [dept_no])
> departments(<u>dept no</u>, location)

5.10 Accommodating Non-Functional Dependencies

We accommodate non-functional dependencies by applying the following rule:

> *Every non-functional determinant becomes part of the primary*
> *key of a table.*

That is, we make up a compound key from the determinant and dependent data-items in a non-functional association.

Suppose we add the data-items skill_code and skill_name to our dataset. Whereas skill_code functionally determines skill_name, employee_number non-functionally determines skill_code. This leads to the amended diagram in figure 5.7

How many tables do we now need? We need three tables to represent the functional dependencies *employee_no - employee_name*, *dept_no - location* and *skill_code - skill_name*. We also need a table to record the multi-valued dependency between *employee_no* and *skill_code* (see figure 5.8). This gives us four table-structures as below:

> employees(<u>employee no</u>, employee_name, [dept_no])
> departments(<u>dept no</u>, location)
> skills(<u>skill code</u>, skill_name)
> employee_skills([<u>employee number</u>], [<u>skill code</u>])

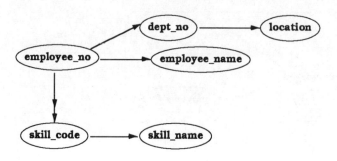

Figure 5.7

Note how *employee_no* and *skill_code* have been declared not null foreign keys in the table *employee_skills*. We could have left the square brackets off the data-items in this case since they both form part of a primary key and no part of a primary key may be null.

5.11 Candidate Keys

A determinancy diagram is useful in identifying candidate keys. A candidate key is any data-item that can act in the capacity of a primary key for a table. In determinancy diagramming terms candidate keys are represented by competing determinants. Consider the diagram in figure 5.9. Here both *employee_no* and national insurance number (*NI_no*) de-

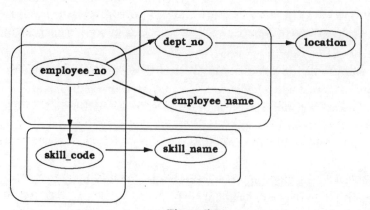

Figure 5.8

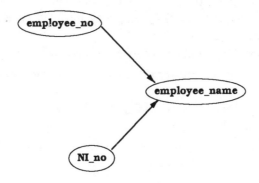

Figure 5.9

termine *employee_name* independently. In this case, *employee_no* and *NI_no* are candidate keys. We choose one of these to be the actual key of the table and make the other a dependent data-item in the table.

5.12 Advantages of Determinancy Diagramming

The main advantage of the determinancy diagramming technique is that it provides a mechanism for designing a database incrementally. One does not need a complete data-set in hand to begin the process of design. The data analyst can begin his work with a small collection of central data-items. Around this core data-items can be continuously added until the dependencies are fully documented.

Since accommodation from a set of dependencies is now a straightforward process subject to formal rules a number of CAISE tools are available which automate this process. Such tools will be discussed in chapter 14.

5.13 Determinancy Diagramming and the Normal Forms

In this section we shall connect up the discussion on non-loss decomposition with our discussion of determinancy diagramming.

First, second and third normal forms are all about functional dependencies.

First normal form concerns repeating groups. Since functional dependencies document one to many relationships between data they are an explicit representation of repeating groups. Second normal form concerns part-key dependencies. Here we are segmenting functional dependencies out from a compound key. Third normal form concerns inter-data dependencies. Here we are identifying determinants within the non-key attributes of a table.

Fourth and fifth normal forms are about multi-valued dependencies.

Fourth normal form concerns independent multi-valued dependencies. Figure 5.10 represents a determinancy diagram for the problem discussed in section 4.11. Here *employee_no* multi-value determines *skill* and *language* independently. If however we relax the independence assumption then the diagram will look as in figure 5.11. One table, rather than two, will now suffice as a storage structure.

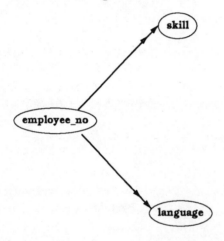

Figure 5.10

Fifth normal form concerns so-called join dependencies. Figure 5.12 documents the assertions for the problem described in section 4.12, namely, the assertion that each agent sells only some products for some companies. If we rewrite the assertion as an agent represents some company, a company makes some products, an agent sells some products then our determinancy diagram changes (see figure 5.12). We now need three tables to store this structure.

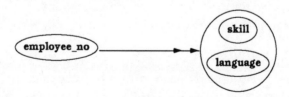

Figure 5.11

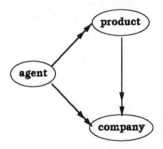

Figure 5.12

5.14 Daley's Cars Reviewed

We refresh the discussion by reviewing Daley's Cars. Rather than conducting the normalisation process in a step-by-step manner we now document all the dependencies as in figure 5.13. All the dependencies can then be combined to give us the complete picture as in figure 5.14. Performing the accommodation process we arrive at the following table structures:

Bodies(<u>model</u>, <u>style</u>, market)
Markets(<u>market</u>, main_competitor)
Cars(<u>model</u>, <u>style</u>, <u>engine</u>, price)
Engines(<u>engine</u>, capacity)

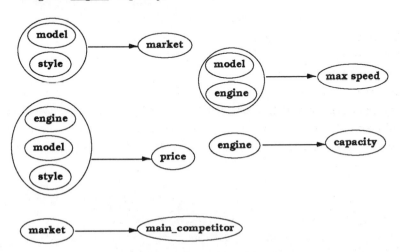

Figure 5.13

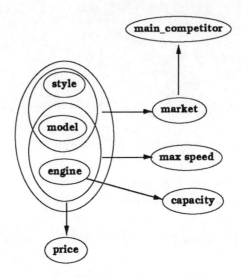

Figure 5.14

Performance(<u>model</u>, <u>engine</u>, max_speed)

5.15 Conclusion

In this chapter we have described a pragmatic approach to bottom-up data analysis. It is pragmatic in the sense that it applies an iterative diagramming and accommodation process to the problem of normalisation.

The end-result of normalisation is a relational schema: a logical design for a relational database. In the next two chapters we discuss a top-down approach to achieving the same end-result.

5.16 Exercises

(1) Discuss the distinction between a determinant and dependent data-item.

(2) Distinguish between functional determinancy and non-functional determinancy.

(3) What is accommodation?

(4) How is determinancy diagramming related to the normal forms?

(5) Describe what is meant by the bracketing notation.

(6) Draw a determinancy diagram for each of the following types of marriage:

(a) monogamy- one man marries one woman;

(b) polygamy - one man can marry many women, but every woman marries a single man;

(c) polyandry - one woman can marry many men, but every man marries a single woman;

(d) group marriage - one man can marry many women, one woman can marry many men.

(7) Accommodate each dependency diagram in 6 above into a relational schema expressed in the bracketing notation.

(8) Draw a determinancy diagram from the table below. Convert the determinancy diagram into a set of table structures.

Practice Name	Doctor Name	Infant NHS_no	Infant Name	Parent NHS_no	Vaccination Code	Vaccine Name
Ystrad	J Thomas	12456	Jenkins	14534	1523	Mumps
Ystrad	J Thomas	25643	Thomas	22223	1524	Mumps
Ystrad	D Evans	43256	Jenkins	14534	1525	Mumps
Ystrad	D Evans	43256	Jenkins	14534	1425	Polio
Pentre	P Davies	33445	Evans	38976	1626	Polio
Pentre	P Davies	42389	Davies	22447	1627	Polio
Pentre	P Davies	42389	Davies	22447	1342	Rubella
Pentre	I Jones	33129	Howells	35612	1324	Rubella
Treorci	F Evans	32445	Evans	30976	1726	Polio
Treorci	T Davies	42386	Davies	20447	1727	Polio
Treorci	T Davies	42589	Jones	22407	1742	Rubella
Treorci	L Evans	33029	Jones	30612	1724	Rubella

(9) Annotate the table structures given in section 5.14 with suitable foreign key specifications.

Chapter 6
Top-Down Data Analysis:
The Fundamentals

6.1 Introduction

In this chapter we describe in some detail the top-down approach to data analysis. In the bottom-up approach we must have a data-set in place before we can begin the process of database design. The aim of bottom-up data analysis is to divide this data-set into logical groupings. Bottom-up data analysis is therefore concrete data analysis.

In contrast, top-down data analysis is data analysis in the abstract. There is no data-set in place which we can examine. Instead, we have to build a model of the 'things of interest' to an organisation. Such a model is usually referred to as an entity model.

6.2 Entity Models

Top-down data analysis involves modelling some aspect of the real world in terms of entity models. An entity model is a representation of some universe of discourse in terms of entities and relationships.

There are a number of ways we can build an entity model. In chapter 8, for instance, we will demonstrate how an entity model can be represented as a meta-database known as a data dictionary. In this chapter, however, we will use a graphic technique known as entity-relationship diagramming (E-R diagramming) to document our entity models. Figure 6.1 illustrates a simple E-R diagram.

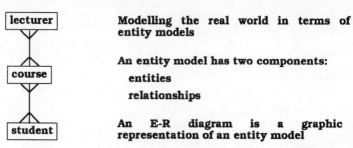

Modelling the real world in terms of entity models

An entity model has two components:
   entities
   relationships

An E-R diagram is a graphic representation of an entity model

Figure 6.1

First however, we need to define the two parts of any entity model: entities and relationships.

6.3 Entities

An entity is a 'thing of interest' to some organisation. When we speak of an entity we normally speak of some aspect of the real world which can be distinguished from other aspects of the real world.

To be accurate, our definition of entities above is really a definition of entity types. An entity type is a category or concept which defines entities. Hence, person is an entity type whereas Paul Beynon-Davies is an instance of this entity type. Paul Beynon-Davies is an entity.

The term object has become fashionable in recent times. Although, as we shall discuss in chapter 9, this is not a totally correct analogy, entities can be regarded as being more or less synonymous with objects. Entity types are synonymous with classes of objects.

Because the term entity type is somewhat cumbersome, most people tend to use the term entity as a synonym. We shall conform to this practice throughout this work. It must be remembered however that when we speak of an entity we actually mean an entity type.

Entities are by their very nature *interesting things* because entities are normally used to define logical data groupings (see figure 6.2). In conven-

 **ENTITY TYPE** A thing which some organisation recognises as being capable of independent existence and which can be uniquely identified

Normally defines a data group: a set of data items/attributes

PERSON	DEPT	GRADE	POSITION
person_no	dept_no	grade_code	position
name	name	description	description
address	division	vacation	dept_no
grade_code	location	days	min_yrs.
service	manager	company	min_educ
department		car	level
date_of_birth		profit	
date_joined		scheme	

Figure 6.2

tional information processing jargon the term logical data grouping normally means a file. One rule of thumb to apply in identifying suitable entities for a given application is therefore the following:

> *If you need to store data about many properties of some thing, then that thing is likely to be an entity.*

6.4 Diversity of Notational Devices

There is unfortunately no standard notation for E-R diagramming. All of the conventions in figure 6.3, for instance, have been used by various persons. In this work we shall employ a notation based upon a set of standards proposed by Martin (Martin and McClure, 1985). Our major intent has been to provide a consistent practice for moving between top-down and bottom-up data analysis. Hence, squares or rectangles are always used for entities, whereas circles or ovals are always used for data items or attributes.

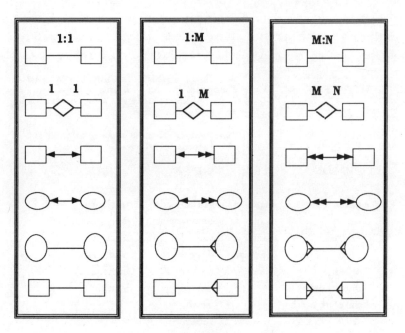

Figure 6.3

6.5 A Graphic for Entities

We indicate an entity on our entity model by drawing a labelled box. Figure 6.4 illustrates eight different entities of relevance to information systems. *Patient, car* and *customer* are all physical entities. They have some concrete existence in the real world. *Appointment* and *consultation* are event entities. They have no concrete existence as such, but serve to organise events in the real world. *Invoice, statement* and *order* are abstract entities. They are classic instruments of business practice.

Note that in each case we label the entity with a singular noun. We speak of an order and not of orders, a patient and not of patients. This is because an entity represents a category of something. There is only one instance of a category.

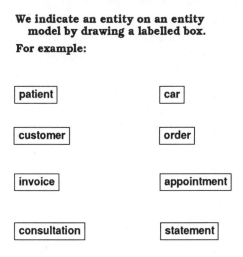

We indicate an entity on an entity model by drawing a labelled box.
For example:

patient	car
customer	order
invoice	appointment
consultation	statement

Figure 6.4

6.6 Brightholmlee General Hospital

Figure 6.5 documents in summary form an environment at a general hospital in the UK. Our first task is to identify the entities in the proposed system.

Most of the entities identified in figure 6.6 are fairly clear-cut. We would probably need to store information on doctors, patients, clinics, and theatres. These are all physical entities. We would also however like to

The Brightholmlee General Hospital deals
with patients using an appointments
system. Patients must make an
appointment for a clinic session held at one
of the hospital's clinics.

Doctors are allocated one or more
appointments within a clinic session, but
only one doctor will be present at each
appointment.

Operations are scheduled and allocated to
one of a number of theatre sessions held in
the hospital's operating theatres. Each
doctor may perform a number of given
operations on patients.

Figure 6.5

store information about important events: sessions, appointments, and
operations (see figure 6.6).

Note that we have not included the hospital itself as an entity. This is
because it represents just one instance of something. There is not much
point in having a file with just one record in it. If however this was a
regional or even a national system then hospital would probably become
an entity. It would then have many possible instances. Hence, another
rule of thumb for identifying entities is:

*If something has many instances or examples then that thing is
probably an entity.*

The Brightholmlee General Hospital deals
with patients using an appointments
system. Patients must make an
appointment for a clinic session held at one
of the hospital's clinics.

Doctors are allocated one or more
appointments within a clinic session, but
only one doctor will be present at each
appointment.

Operations are scheduled and allocated to
one of a number of theatre sessions held in
the hospital's operating theatres. Each
doctor may perform a number of given
operations on patients.

Figure 6.6

6.7 Relationship

A relationship is some association between entities. In this chapter we shall concentrate on binary relationships. That is, associations between two entities. In chapter 6 we shall introduce other N-ary relationships. That is, relationships between one, three, four or N entities.

In terms of the relational data model we shall see that a relationship is present if some attribute is common to two data groups. Hence, the entities grade and employee might be related via the attribute grade code.

More than one relationship can exist between two entities. Consider, for instance, the entities house and person. A house can be owned by a person and/or occupied by a person. Hence, in a student town many houses will be merely occupied by students. Landlords will usually own such houses.

Between any N entities there are 1/2N(N-1) possible relationships between such entities. Suppose we have four entities: doctor, patient, appointment and clinic. Theoretically there are six possible binary relationships between such entities. In practice however, many of these relationships would be classed as being unimportant or as indirect relationships (see figure 6.7).

An indirect relationship is one that can be fulfilled by other relationships in an entity model. Take the three entities parent, child and school.

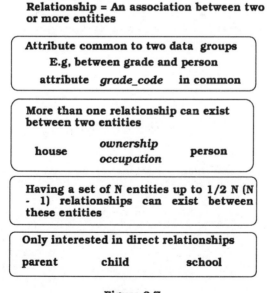

Relationship = An association between two or more entities

Attribute common to two data groups
E.g, between grade and person
attribute *grade_code* in common

More than one relationship can exist between two entities
house *ownership* person
occupation

Having a set of N entities up to 1/2 N (N - 1) relationships can exist between these entities

Only interested in direct relationships
parent child school

Figure 6.7

A parent is related to both children and schools. Likewise a child is related to parents and schools. Hence, everything in this entity model is related to everything else. One of these relationships however might in some circumstances be considered indirect. Parent to school, for instance, might be represented by the relationships parent-child and child-school.

Note however that we must be clear about what we are attempting to represent. If the relationship between parent and child is one of parenting, the relationship between child and school is one of child attends school, and the relationship between parent and school is one of parent chooses school to send child then the parent-school relationship is probably correctly labelled as an indirect relationship. Consider however the case of the relationship between parent and school being parent is governor of school. This is no longer an indirect relationship. It cannot be represented by the two relationships parent-child and child-school. Not every parent of a child is a school governor (see figure 6.7).

6.8 A Notation for Relationships

We indicate a relationship on an entity model by drawing a line between two boxes representing entities (see figure 6.8). In some notations labels are placed on the relationship lines. This is a useful technique in resolving

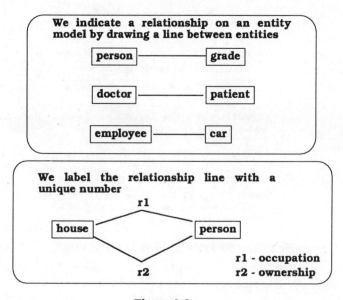

Figure 6.8

ambiguity. There are however a number of problems with this convention:

(1) It is frequently difficult to think of a meaningful label for relationships.

(2) Most relationships are best represented by verbs. Verbs however
usually imply some direction. Hence the relationship between person
and grade might be read as person is graded by grade in one direction
and grade grades person in the opposite direction. This is cumbersome.

In this text we shall therefore adopt the practice of labelling relationships with a simple numbering convention. We assign to each relationship
on our entity model a unique number. This number is then used to
reference an entry in a data dictionary. We shall delay this discussion until
chapter 8.

Figure 6.9 indicates the entities identified as relevant to the appointments system of Brightholmlee hospital.

The Brightholmlee General Hospital deals with patients
using an appointments system. Patients must make an
appointment for a clinic session held at one of the
hospital's clinics.

Doctors are allocated one or more appointments within
a clinic session, but only one doctor will be present at
each appointment.

Operations are scheduled and allocated to one of a
number of theatre sessions held in the hospital's
operating theatres. Each doctor may perform a number
of given operations on patients.

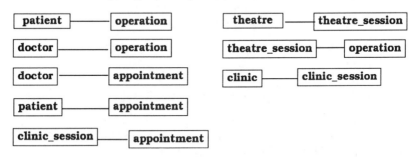

Figure 6.9

6.9 Properties of a Relationship

A number of properties of a relationship are conventionally regarded as
being important. These properties are known by various names: degree or

cardinality and participation or optionality are some of the most popular. We choose to call them cardinality and participation.

6.10 Cardinality of a Relationship

Cardinality relates the number of instances of each entity involved in a relationship. A relationship can be said to be in one of three states of cardinality: one-to-one (1:1); one-to-many (1:M); many-to-many (M:N).

Figure 6.10 illustrates how the assertions associated with a relationship change as the cardinality of the relationship changes.

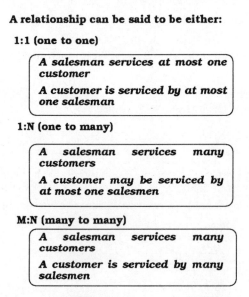

A relationship can be said to be either:

1:1 (one to one)

> *A salesman services at most one customer*
>
> *A customer is serviced by at most one salesman*

1:N (one to many)

> *A salesman services many customers*
>
> *A customer may be serviced by at most one salesmen*

M:N (many to many)

> *A salesman services many customers*
>
> *A customer is serviced by many salesmen*

Figure 6.10

6.11 A Notation for Cardinality

There are many ways of representing cardinality. We choose to represent cardinality by drawing a crows-foot at the many end of a relationship. Hence, in a many-to-many relationship there are two crows-feet, in a one-to-many one crows-foot, and in a one-to-one relationship no crows-feet. Figure 6.11a represents a 1:1 relationship, 6.11b and c are 1:M relationships, and 6.11d and e are M:N relationships. Figure 6.12 indicates the likely cardinality for the relationships at Brightholmlee.

We indicate cardinality on an entity model by drawing a crow's-foot on the many end of a relationship

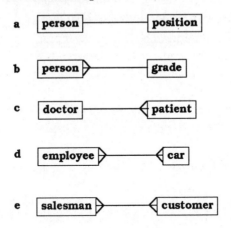

Figure 6.11

6.12 Participation

The second property we wish to document in our entity model is the participation of each entity in their associated relationships. Participation is about exceptions. There are two states of participation: mandatory and optional.

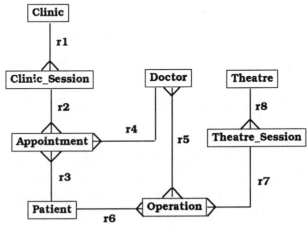

Figure 6.12

We say that an entity has mandatory participation in the relationship if every instance of an entity is associated with the relationship. In contrast, we say that an entity has optional participation if at least one instance of an entity is not involved in a relationship.

Hence in the assertions given below the entity employee has mandatory status while the entity department is optionally involved in the relationship.

Every employee must be employed within a department
A department may exist without any employees

6.13 Venn Diagrams

Figure 6.13 and 6.14 illustrate two Venn diagrams. The circles or ovals on the diagrams are meant to represent sets. Each entity therefore is represented here as a set of instances. A line drawn between instances of two sets indicates a specific instance of a relationship. Hence, in figure 6.13 the line drawn between E3 and D3 indicates that employee E3 is employed by department D3.

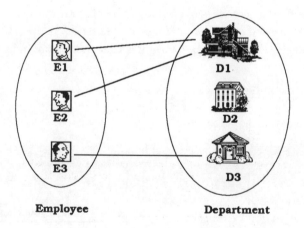

Employee   **Department**

Figure 6.13

Note that the cardinality of the relationship in figure 6.13 is 1:M. Department D1, for instance, has two employees associated with it. Employee has mandatory participation while department has optional participation. D2, for instance, is not associated with any employees.

In figure 6.14 *salesman* to *customer* is a many-to-many relationship.

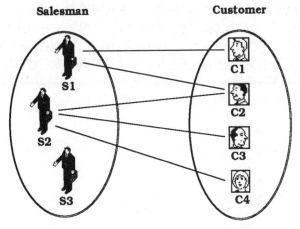

(<S1,C1>,<S1,C2>,<S2,C3>,<S3,C4>)

Figure 6.14

Salesman S1, for example, services customers C1 and C2, while customer C2 is serviced both by salesman S1 and salesman S2. The entity *salesman* is optional since S3 is not involved in the relationship.

6.14 A Notation for Participation

When an entity's participation is optional, we draw a circle ('O' for optional) outside the entity symbol on the relationship line next to the entity. An entity's participation is assumed by default to be mandatory. Hence, if no circle appears next to the entity symbol then this indicates mandatory participation (see figure 6.15).

When an entity's participation is optional we draw a circle on the relationship line outside the entity symbol

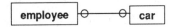

When an entity's participation is mandatory we leave off the circle

Figure 6.15

Figure 6.16 assigns some sensible participation to each of the entities in the Brightholmlee hospital system. Note that there is not enough information supplied to be entirely sure of an appropriate answer. The problem therefore calls for the analyst to make assumptions. This is one more benefit of the process of entity modelling. It is a useful technique for making many information system assumptions explicit.

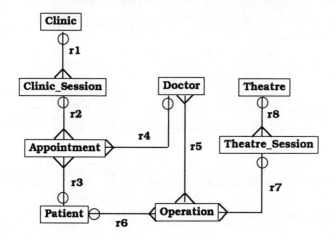

Figure 6.16

6.15 Indemnity Insurance

In the preceding sections of this chapter we have introduced the concept of entity modelling and demonstrated a particular graphic technique for entity modelling known as entity-relationship diagramming. In this section we consolidate the concepts learned by applying them to one small example.

Suppose, for instance, our task is to build a database system for a major national insurance company called Indemnity Insurance. Figure 6.17 lists some seven paragraphs which document the assertions of this universe of discourse. The task of the data analyst is to turn these assertions into an entity model for the business.

We approach the problem systematically and begin by listing what we feel to be the major entities of the business. A suggested list is given below:

policy-holder, policy, product, broker, claim, claim-type, business-area, association, reinsurer, commission

A policy-holder may have a number of policies with the company. Each policy is given a policy number and relates to a single holder

The company has a range of products and may put together a number of products to form a policy sold to a holder. Examples of motor products are:

> *third party, fire, theft, accident
> damage, windscreen cover etc.*

Brokers sell policies for commission and any one policy may have commission payable to more than one broker

Claims are made against policies. A claim relates to only one policy and each claim is classified according to one of six claim types

The company's products are grouped by business area, ie., life, motor, marine etc. Any particular product belongs to only one business area

The company holds information on clubs and associations, for promotions and selective mailings. A holder may belong to a number of different associations

In order to limit risk the company may place all or part of a policy with re-insurers. All or part of a single policy may be placed with a number of different re-insurers

Create an E-R diagram to represent the system at Indemnity Insurance

Figure 6.17

Next we list relationships between entities as below:

policy-holder - policy

broker - policy

claim - policy

policy - product

claim - policy

business-area - product

association - policy-holder

reinsurer - policy

broker - commission

policy - commission

Then we add an assumed cardinality for each of these relationships as in figure 6.18. Finally, we add an appropriate participation for each entity in each relationship as in figure 6.19.

It cannot be over-emphasised that each binary relationship between entities represents a business rule. Hence, the diagram of the relationship between holder and policy represents the following assertions:

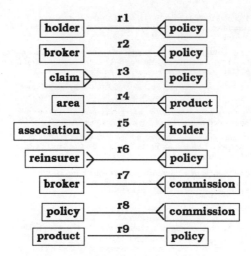

Figure 6.18

Each holder may have many insurance policies.
Each policy is associated with only one holder.
Every policy must have a holder associated with it.
Every holder must have at least one policy.

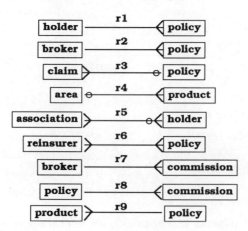

Figure 6.19

A full understanding of any entity model cannot be achieved completely until all the aspects of the model are drawn on one diagram. Only with one diagram can we see all the inter-relationships between entities. Only with one diagram can we ask questions about the minimality of the model. Figure 6.20 represents such a diagram.

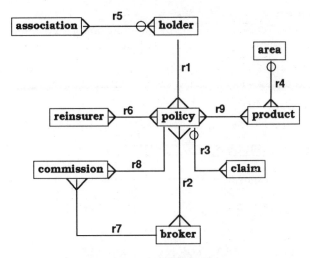

Figure 6.20

One way we might simplify our entity model is by examining the relationships between policy, commission and broker. Are these relationships identical to the many -to-many relationship between policy and broker? If they are, we can delete this relationship from our diagram. If they are not, then we have to assume that this represents a distinct relationship from that of commission.

6.16 Conclusion

In this chapter we have considered the fundamentals of top-down data analysis. We have introduced entity models via a graphic technique known as entity-relationship diagramming. In the next chapter we extend this discussion by considering some of the practicalities associated with this technique. The aim is to discuss some of the subtleties of top-down data analysis, and, in particular, to discuss how a relational schema is produced.

6.17 Exercises

(1) What is an entity model?
(2) Define an entity.
(3) Define a relationship.
(4) Define an attribute.
(5) How many types of cardinality can we associate with relationships?

(6) What is optionality or participation?

(7) How are Venn diagrams useful in understanding cardinality and participation?

(8) See figure 6.21.

(9) Write the assertions associated with the relationship between holder and policy in figure 6.20.

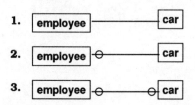

SELECT THE MOST APPROPRIATE E-R DIAGRAM TO REPRESENT THE STATEMENT BELOW:

Employees do not necessarily have company cars, and cars, perhaps those newly acquired, are not necessarily used by company employees.

Figure 6.21

Chapter 7
Entity-Relationship Diagramming:
Pragmatics

7.1 Introduction

In the previous chapter we discussed the fundamentals of entity modelling as expressed in the technique of entity-relationship diagramming. In this chapter we continue our discussion of the top-down approach to data analysis by looking at some practical issues surrounding the use of E-R diagramming as a design technique.

7.2 Adding Attributes

As a real-world aspect, an entity is characterised by a number of properties or attributes. Figure 7.1 illustrates how attributes can be added to an entity model. Following the notation we introduced in chapter 6, each attribute is drawn as a labelled oval and associated with its particular entity. We also choose one or more attributes to act as identifiers for instances of an entity. Hence, *holder_no* has been chosen as an identifier for the *holder* entity and *policy_no* as an identifier for the *policy* entity. We indicate identifiers on E-R diagrams by underlining the attribute name.

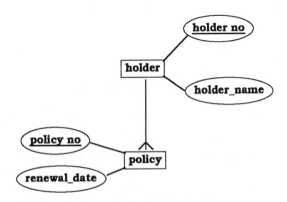

Figure 7.1

7.3 E-R Diagrams and Determinancy Diagrams

There is a correspondence between the diagramming technique we have
used for bottom-up design and the technique we are using for top-down
design. Take, for instance, part of our entity model for Indemnity Insurance. A one-to-many relationship between *holder* and *policy* on our E-R
diagram corresponds to a functional dependency between the identifiers
policy_no and *holder_no* on our determinancy diagram. All other attributes
of the entity *holder* are dependent on the identifying attribute *holder_no*.
Similarly, all other attributes of the entity *policy* are dependent on the
attribute *policy_no*. This is illustrated in figure 7.2.

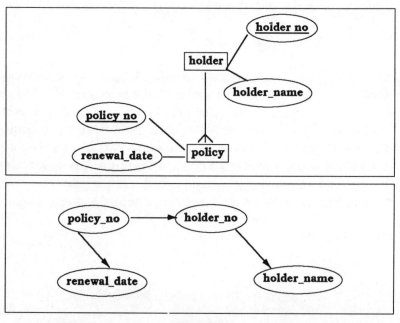

Figure 7.2

7.4 Simplifying Many-to-Many Relationships

To simplify the process of accommodating to a relational schema we shall
recommend decomposing any many-to-many relationship in an entity
model into two one-to-many relationships. Figure 7.3 illustrates a many-
to-many relationship between *policy* and *broker*. To decompose this relationship we introduce a link entity which we choose to call *brokerage*. This
entity now cross-refers between instances of the *broker* entity and in-

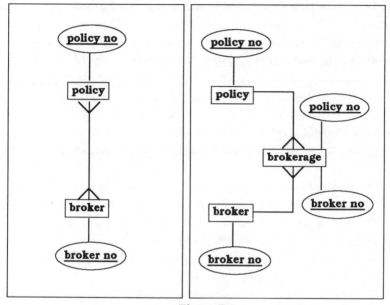

Figure 7.3

stances of the *policy* entity. A particular *policy_no* will occur a number of times in the *brokerage* entity, as will a particular *broker_no*. The identifier for the link entity is therefore made up of a compound of the identifiers of the two original entities: *broker_no* and *policy_no*.

Figure 7.4 illustrates how the breakdown of a many-to-many relation-

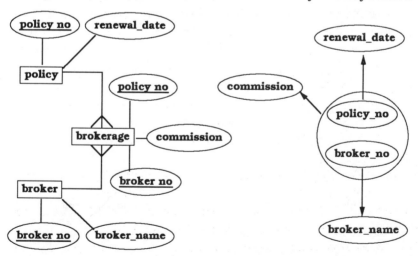

Figure 7.4

ship corresponds to a non-functional dependency between identifying attributes. Note we have chosen to represent these attributes as a compound key because of their role in determining other attributes such as *commission, renewal_date* and *broker_name*.

7.5 Accommodating Entity-Relationship Diagrams

Given the simplification we made in section 7.4, the process of accommodating an entity model to a relational schema is relatively straightforward.

(1) For each entity on our diagram we form a table. It is conventional to take each entity name and make it a plural. Hence from the entity model in figure 7.5 we arrive at two tables: *policies* and *holders*.

(2) The identifying attribute of the entity becomes the primary key of the table. *Policy_no* and *holder_no* become the primary keys of *holders* and *policies* respectively.

(3) All other attributes of an entity become non-key attributes of the table. *Renewal_date* is a non-key attribute of *policies*. *Holder_name* is a non-key attribute of *holders*.

(4) For each one-to-many relationship, post the primary key of the one table into the table representing the many end of the relationship. Hence we post *holder_no* into the *policies* table.

(5) Optionality on the many end of a relationship tells us whether the foreign key representing the relationship can be null or not. If the many end is mandatory the foreign key cannot be null. If the foreign key is optional the foreign key can be null. In figure 7.5A *holder_no* cannot be null. In figure 7.5B *holder_no* can be null.

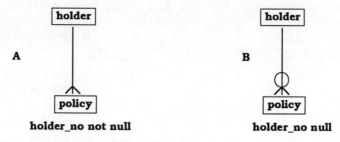

policies(<u>policy no</u>, renewal_date, holder_no,....)
holders(<u>holder no</u>, holder_name,....)

Figure 7.5

Note that we have not considered many-to-many or one-to-one relationships in the accommodation process described above. Many-to-many relationships we assume will be broken down into one-to-many relationships. One-to-one relationships can normally be handled as a single table. In other words, we take both entities and feed the attributes into one table structure. There are some exceptions to this rule which we will consider in chapter 13.

7.6 One Man's Entity

> *One man's entity is another man's relationship*
> *One man's entity is another man's attribute*
> *One man's relationship is another man's attribute*
> *and so on ...*

This corruption of a popular adage is true of entity modelling because entity modelling is the modelling of semantics. Our aim in drawing an E-R diagram is to represent the meaning associated with some aspect of the real world.

Let us assume, for instance, that we wish to represent some of the information stored by the marriage registry as an E-R diagram. There are a number of ways we can model this aspect of the world using E-R constructs (see figure 7.6).

One man's attribute is another man's entity and one man's entity is another man's relationship.

E.G., MARRIAGE

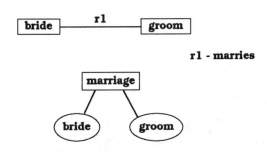

Figure 7.6

We can, for example, make *bride* and *groom* entities and document a *marries* relationship between these two entities. Alternatively, the act of *marriage* could be an entity with *bride* and *groom* delegated to the status of attributes.

How then do we choose which of these representations is the most appropriate one for our purposes? One rule to follow is to assign priorities to the three E-R constructs: entities, relationships and attributes. Top priority is given to entities, least priority is given to attributes and median priority is given to relationships.

> *If something is of fundamental importance to your application, then model it as an entity. If something is of lesser importance, then model it as an attribute.*

7.7 Validating Entity Models

We now come to the process of validation - the activity by which we validate an entity model against a set of processing requirements. In figure 7.7, for instance, we list some six requirements that the entity model for Indemnity Insurance should fulfill. Note that these are all regular queries that must be run on the database. Our task is to check these off, one at a time, against our data model.

Retrieve details of all policies associated with a particular holder, giving details of products, claims and brokers.

Produce a list of all holders that belong to a particular association.

For a broker retrieve details of all policies and associated holders, products and claims.

List all policies that have been all or part 'laid-off' with a particular reinsurer.

A facility for selecting all policies due for renewal on a particular date.

A faciltity for listing claims by claim type.

Validate these requirements against the entity model.

Figure 7.7

Figure 7.8 illustrates how we conduct such a validation exercise for the first requirement in our list. The entrance for this query into our entity model will be at the *holder* entity. We can confirm that the one-to-many relationship between *holder* and *policy* will give us all policies associated with a particular holder. Since *policy* is a central entity we can also confirm that we can retrieve details of brokers, claims and products.

Note that we have to be careful not to fall into some notable traps in entity modelling. These will be discussed in the next section.

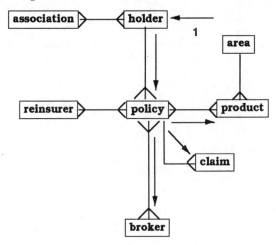

1. Retrieve details of all policies associated with a particular holder,
   giving details of products, claims and brokers.

Figure 7.8

7.8 Connection Traps

Figures 7.9 to 7.11 illustrate a number of potential pitfalls in entity modelling. These pitfalls are known as connection traps because they make invalid asumptions about the connection between entities (Howe, 1986).

Figure 7.9 illustrates a type of connection trap known as a fan trap. This entity model documents the following assertions about the application:

A division has many departments.
Every department belongs to at most one division.

A division has many employees.
An employee belongs to at most one division.

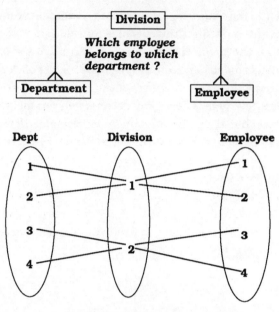

Figure 7.9

The database designer assumed that this organisation was sufficient to tell him which employees belong to which departments. As we see from the associated venn diagram however this assumption is incorrect. Although we can tell from the entity model which employee belongs to which department and which department belongs to which division, the link between employees and departments is ambiguous.

Figure 7.10 illustrates a representation for the same entity model which

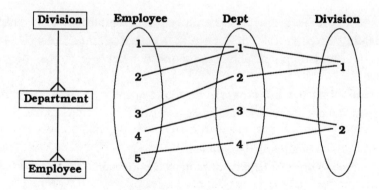

Figure 7.10

overcomes the fan trap. The venn diagram makes clear that the query - *which employees work for which departments* - is clearly answerable from this revised model.

This revised model may however be subject to a further problem. What if we have in our company employees who are employed by divisions rather than by departments? Our entity model would give us an incorrect answer as it assumes that all employees must be employed by departments. This is known as a chasm trap. To fulfill this new requirement we have to introduce an additional relationship on our diagram between employee and division (see figure 7.11).

Note that what defines a fan trap or a chasm trap is determined by the semantics of the application. Figure 7.10, for instance, would be perfectly reasonable as a representation of some applications where the business rules prohibit divisional employees.

What if we have divisional employees?

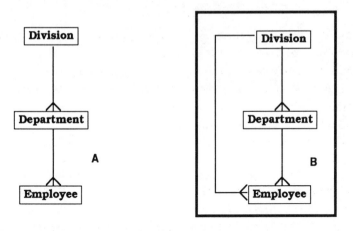

Figure 7.11

7.9 Modelling Time

Most database systems exist within a temporal dimension. This is because most database systems handle events - real-world entities that must be time-stamped. In this section we discuss some techniques for including past and future time in our database design.

Consider the case where a technical training company wants to build a database recording details of the courses it runs and details of the persons who attend such courses. The simplest solution to their problem is to model courses and attendees in a time-independent way. In other words, we maintain information only about courses currently running and the attendees presently on such courses. This means that we model the relationship between *attendee* and *course* as a one-to-many relationship. Similarly, we model the dependency between identifiers as a functional dependency (see figure 7.12). Using this approach an attendee is recorded on our database as attending at most one course.

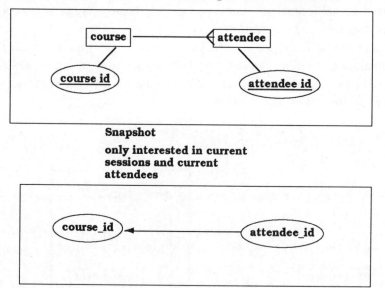

Snapshot

only interested in current sessions and current attendees

Figure 7.12

A more realistic situation is approached when the training company decides it wishes to store information about past course events. We now wish to record which attendees have attended which courses over a period of say five years. This is useful for the company to help them determine which attendees/companies regularly use their training courses. We now make the relationship between *course* and *attendee* a many-to-many relationship. Many attendees can attend many different courses over a period of time.

In accordance with our practice we create a link entity which decomposes this many-to-many relationship. Attendance is an entity which records which attendees have been on which courses (see figure 7.13).

This structure however is equally capable of handling future events. Suppose the company wishes to extend the use of its database to schedule

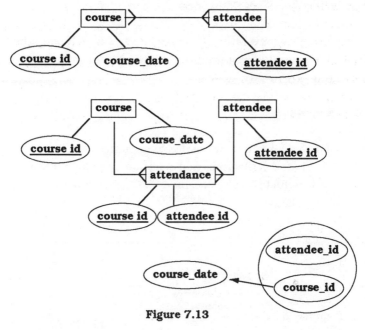

Figure 7.13

future courses. The only modification we need to make to our entity model is to make course and attendee optional in the appropriate relationships. In other words, we wish to allow course details to be recorded prior to places being filled. Likewise we wish to record details of attendees prior to their attendance on a particular course.

7.10 Conclusion

In this chapter we have considered the following practical issues surrounding the use of entity modelling as embodied in E-R diagramming as a top-down database design technique:

(1) Adding attributes.
(2) The relationship between E-R diagrams and determinancy diagrams.
(3) Simplifying many-to-many relationships.
(4) Accommodating an E-R diagram to a relational schema.
(5) The importance of recognising entity modelling as a process of modelling semantics.
(6) Validating entity models against processing requirements.
(7) Identifying connection traps.

(8) Modelling time in entity models.

An entity model is conventionally represented as an E-R diagram. In the next chapter we study an alternative, non-graphic technique designed for documenting large entity models.

7.11 Exercises

(1) In what way are attributes added to an entity model?

(2) Describe how E-R diagrams and determinancy diagrams are related.

(3) Why is it useful to break down many-to-many relationships into one-to-many relationships?

(4)

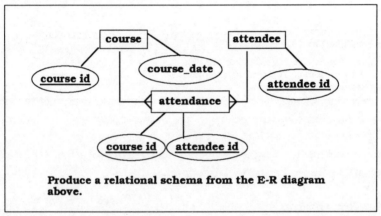

Produce a relational schema from the E-R diagram above.

(5) Break down all the many-to-many relationships in the Indemnity Insurance entity model.

(6) Describe what is meant by a fan trap and chasm trap.

(7)

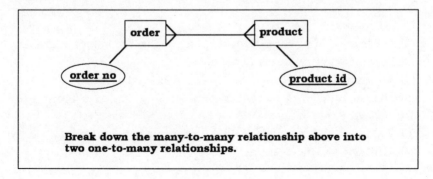

Break down the many-to-many relationship above into two one-to-many relationships.

(8) How is time handled in entity models?

(9)

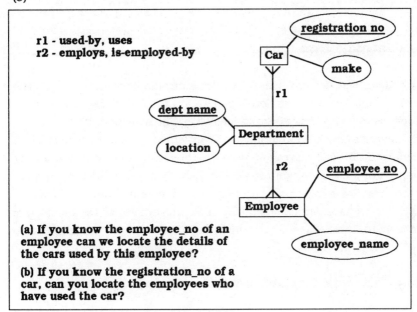

r1 - used-by, uses
r2 - employs, is-employed-by

(a) If you know the employee_no of an employee can we locate the details of the cars used by this employee?

(b) If you know the registration_no of a car, can you locate the employees who have used the car?

Chapter 8
Data Dictionaries

8.1 Introduction

In chapter 6 we defined an entity model as any model of the real world built out of entities and relationships. An entity model however can be represented in a number of different ways. The most popular representation is certainly entity-relationship diagramming. One of the main problems with an E-R diagram however is that as it gets more detailed the efficacy of the technique starts to diminish. As more entities and relationships are drawn, diagrams become less easy to understand and manipulate. For this reason, it is usual for practising data analysts to exploit an alternative mechanism for documenting entity models. That mechanism is the data dictionary.

8.2 What is a data dictionary?

A data dictionary is a means for recording the metadata of some organisation. That is, data about data. Data dictionaries have been conventionally used in two ways:

(1) Logical data dictionaries are used to record data requirements independently of how these requirements are to be met.
(2) Physical data dictionaries are used to record design decisions. That is, in terms of actual database or file structures.

In terms of metadata therefore we conventionally mean both data resources and data requirements. A data dictionary is a mechanism for recording the data resources and requirements of some organisation. This means that a data dictionary cannot be considered solely as a tool for the analysis and design of database systems. It is also emerging as an important implementation tool and an important function of what we might call the corporate information architecture.

8.3 Active and Passive Data Dictionaries

The classic data dictionary is a passive repository for meta-data. In other words, the first data dictionaries were built as systems external to a database and DBMS. They were systems built to record the complexities of a given database structure for use by application development staff and database administrators (DBAs).

If we equate the term data dictionary with the set of system tables in a relational database, then a data dictionary in a relational system is an active repository. It is an inherent, internal part of the database system designed to buffer the user from the base tables.

Many people believe however that the system tables available in most SQL-based products are inherently limited in functionality (Codd, 1990). In particular, they wish to see the inclusion of some representation of integrity mechanisms within the data dictionary.

Traditionally, integrity issues have been external to the database system. Integrity has primarily been the province of application systems written in languages such as COBOL or C which interact with the database. Programs are written in such languages to validate data entered into the database and ensure that any suitable propagation of results occurs.

Many have argued however that the logical place for integrity is within the domain of the data dictionary under control of the DBMS. The argument is that integrity cannot be divorced from the underlying database. Two or more application systems interacting with one database may enforce integrity differently or inconsistently. Hence, there should be only one central resort for monitoring integrity. Integrity should be the responsibility of the DBA. Mechanisms should be available therefore for the DBA to define and enforce integrity via the DBMS.

Figure 8.1

8.4 Representing Entities

Figure 8.1 illustrates a minimum format for documenting entities modelled for convenience on a file index card. Each card of this type we will refer to as an entity frame. The basic entity frame has two fields. We need a unique name for each of the entities in our entity model. We also need a description which helps to define what we mean by the entity.

Figure 8.1 illustrates how we might fill out this entity frame with detail for one particular entity from a small application. Figure 8.2 illustrates a data dictionary of four frames which represents the entities in this order-processing application.

As the entity model is built up, more detail will be provided on each of

Entity Name: salesman	Entity Name: customer
Description:	Description:
A company employee whose job is to service existing customers and seek out new customers.	A sole trader who has placed at least one order with the company. Normally a greengrocer or small supermarket.

Entity Name: product	Entity Name: supplier
Description:	Description:
A type of packaged foodstuff bundled for sale to small retailers	A major distributor of foodstuff. A company with which we have placed at least one purchase order.

Figure 8.2

the entity frames. We might include, for instance, details about attributes associated with each of the entities. We may also distinguish identifying attributes from descriptive attributes. Figure 8.3 illustrates an extended frame entry for the customer entity.

8.5 Representing Relationships

Each relationship in our entity model also needs to be documented. Figure 8.4 illustrates a basic relationship frame which the reader will see is more detailed than the basic entity frame. We indicated in chapter 6 that in our notation we prefer to label relationships with unique identifiers. This allows us to supply a number of convenient names for the relationship,

Entity Name:	Customer
Description:	
A sole trader who has placed at least one order with the company. Normally a greengrocer or small supermarket.	
Identifying Attribute(s) customer number	
Other Attributes	
customer name, customer address, customer telephone number, contact name, contact extension, credit limit	

Figure 8.3

read in each possible direction. For each entity in the relationship we document its name, degree and cardinality. We also provide space for a brief description which may help us to disambiguate references at a later

Relationship Identifier: r1	
Name: supplies, is supplied by	
Entity1: supplier	**Entity2:** product
Degree: M	**Degree:** N
Optionality: O	**Optionality:**
Description: Every product in the company catalogue must have a supplier	

Figure 8.4

date. Figure 8.5 illustrates a data dictionary entry for a number of the relationships in the order processing application.

In some conventions, relationships are allowed to own attributes. This particularly applies to many-to-many relationships. Our practice has been to transform many-to-many relationships into two one-to-many relationships, and therefore disallow relationships from owning attributes. Figure 8.6 however illustrates how we might accommodate attribute

Relationship ID: r1	Relationship ID: r2
Name: supplies,is supplied by	**Name:** services,is serviced by
Entity1: supplier **Entity2:** product	**Entity1:** salesman **Entity2:** customer
Degree: M **Degree:** N	**Degree:** 1 **Degree:** N
Optionality: O **Optionality:**	**Optionality:** **Optionality:**
Description: Every product must have a supplier	**Description:** Every customer must have a salesman assigned

Relationship ID: r3
Name: orders,is ordered by
Entity1: customer **Entity2:** product
Degree: M **Degree:** N
Optionality: O **Optionality:** O
Description: products, customers related via an orders relationship

Figure 8.5

information into our relationship frames. In our convention this type of
frame would eventually form a link entity.

Relationship Identifier: r1
Name: supplies, is supplied by
Description: Every product in the company catalogue must have a supplier
Entity1: supplier **Entity2:** product
Degree: M **Degree:** N
Optionality: O **Optionality:**
Identifying Attribute(s) supplier number, product number
Other Attributes major supplier indicator number of previous orders

Figure 8.6

8.6 Representing Attributes

As we approach a more detailed specifiation we may need to document
information about attributes. Figure 8.7 illustrates a sample data dictionary
entry for an attribute. The main item we document is the attribute's

```
┌─────────────────────────────────────────────┐
│  Attribute Name:  Customer number           │
│ ............................................ │
│  Description:                                │
│   A unique serial number generated by the    │
│   company to identify each of its customers.  │
│ ............................................ │
│  Format:  9999 in the range 0001 - 9999      │
│ ............................................ │
│ ............................................ │
│ ............................................ │
│ ............................................ │
└─────────────────────────────────────────────┘
```

Figure 8.7

format. Here, much in the style of declarations in languages such as COBOL, we use 9s to represent integer positions. We may equally well have specified alphabetics - perhaps As - or alphanumerics - perhaps Xs. We might also specifiy additional constraints such as the ranges of numbers.

All this information will be usefully applied in the definition of domains in the relational model.

```
┌─────────────────────────────────────────────┐
│  Dependency ID:    D1                        │
│  Description:                                │
│  Only one customer number per customer name  │
│                                              │
│  Determinant: customer number                │
│  Dependant:  customer name                   │
│                                              │
│  Type of Dependency:  single-valued          │
│                                              │
└─────────────────────────────────────────────┘
```

Figure 8.8

8.7 Representing Dependencies

Just as relationships of association can be documented between entities in a data dictionary, so can relationships of dependency between attributes. Figure 8.8 illustrates a sample dependency entry. Note how we specifiy the determinant and dependent data items and whether the dependency relationship is single-valued or multi-valued.

8.8 Documenting Integrity Constraints

A number of integrity constraints are inherent to the E-R data model itself. For instance, let us suppose we describe the relationship between the entity *employee* and the entity *department* as being one-to-many from *department* to *employee*. We also add that both entities are mandatory in the employs relationship, then we are explicitly documenting a so-called existence constraint. In other words, a department cannot exist without any employees.

Now take the following constraint:

> *No employee should earn more than his manager*

There is currently no mechanism available for expressing this constraint in the graphic notation of the extended E-R model. This is therefore referred to as an additional constraint. Because of the very diverse nature of additional constraints it is unlikely that we will ever arrive at a satisfactory graphic notation for expressing such constructs (although some attempts have been made, Verheijen and Van Bekkum, 1982). We shall therefore suggest enhancing the non-graphic data dictionary approach in this direction. We propose adding a new type of frame to our meta-base called an integrity constraint frame. An example frame is given in figure 8.9.

Note how we are documenting our additional constraint in a simple specification language based on a formalism well-known in the expert systems area (Beynon-Davies, 1991a). These are known as production or

Rule ID: C1
Specification:
IF worker.salary > manager.salary
THEN manager.salary = worker.salary +
(worker.salary*0.1)
Participating Entities:
Employee (role:manager) (role:worker)

Figure 8.9

IF-THEN rules. To simplify our specification we have also decided to delineate the two types of employee involved in the recursive relationship specified in figure 8.10. These might be considered as the two roles played by *employee* in this relationship.

Note also, we have chosen to specify this additional constraint as a transition constraint. That is, if we find the conditions of our rule to be true we shall cause something to happen to our database. We might equally well have expressed it as a static constraint, i.e., we would merely prohibit an invalid state from happening. This is obviously a matter of policy for the database designer.

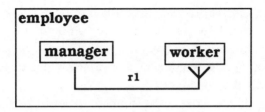

Figure 8.10

8.9 Automating Data Dictionaries

Data dictionaries are inherently associated with both the top-down and bottom-up data analysis techniques discussed in previous chapters. A data dictionary can hence be considered as an integrated repository both for entity-relationship and dependency data. Because of its computational tractability, a data dictionary is particualrly suitable to act as a base representation for the information presented on E-R and determinancy diagrams. In this way, we might envisage an editor for E-R diagramming and an editor for determinancy diagramming as two complementary interfaces to a data dictionary system.This topic will be given more attention in chapter 14.

8.10 Conclusion

In this chapter we have considered an alternative, computationally tractable, representation for entity model and determinancy data. We began by discussing the distinctions between logical and physical data dictionaries and active and passive data dictionaries. We then illustrated some of the mechanisms in a passive data dictionary for representing entities, relationships, attributes and dependencies. We concluded with an examination of the core of a CAISE tool for database deisign.

8.11 Exercises

(1) What is a data dictionary?

(2) Discuss the distinction between a logical and physical data dictionary.

(3) Discuss the distinction between an active and passive data dictionary.

(4) Why are data dictionaries more appropriate mechanisms for documenting large applications than entity-relationship diagrams?

(5) Produce an E-R diagram for the order processing application documented in figures 8.2 and 8.5.

(6) Draw the determinancy diagram for the dependency relationship documented in figure 8.8.

(7) Discuss the distinction betwen inherent and additional constraints.

(8) Categorise each of the following constraints as inherent to the relational data model or additional to the relational data model:

    (a) customer_no uniquely identifies a customer record.

    (b) an order must not be taken until the customer_no is filled

    (c) customer_no should be an integer field of 4 characters in the range 0000 - 9999

    (d) a customer's credit rating should not exceed £5,000

    (e) any customer who has greater than 100 orders outstanding shall be refused further credit

(9) Why are data dictionaries more suitable for specifying additonal constraints than diagrams?

(10) Produce a data dictionary from the E-R diagram for Brightholmlee hospital discussed in chapter 6.

Chapter 9
Extensions to Entity-Relationship Diagramming

9.1 Introduction

Entity-relationship diagramming has undoubtedly become one of the pre-eminent analysis and design techniques in the database area. Created in the mid-1970s, the technique has been the subject of numerous conferences and research papers. As a result, the original data model proposed by P.P.S. Chen has been extended in a number of directions. The overall intention of these extensions has been to provide a consistent approach to modelling aspects of the real world which were not well-handled by the original data model.

This chapter describes some of the most important extensions to this popular data analysis technique.

9.2 Recursive Relationships

In conventional entity-relationship diagrams the relationships are all binary, that is, we diagram two entities and a relationship or a set of relationships between these entities. It is possible however for relationships to be unary, and indeed ternary. In other words, a relationship may involve only a single entity or more than two entities.

Unary relationships are frequently described as being recursive in that they relate entities of the same type. Figures 9.1 and 9.2 detail three relationships and the associated table structures that result from these relationships. In figure 9.1 we have a one-to-one and one-to-many relationship. One employee is married to one other employee; one employee manages many other employees. In figure 9.2a part is documented as containing many other parts, but a part may also be used to assemble a given part. Note how the many-to-many relationship between parts in figure 9.2a is broken down into two one-to-many relationships.

Accommodation to the relational model follows the normal rules for one-to-one, one-to-many and many-to-many relationships. For a one-to-one recursive relationship we normally only need one table. In figure 9.1, *empno* is defined as the primary key of the table. *Partner* is defined on the

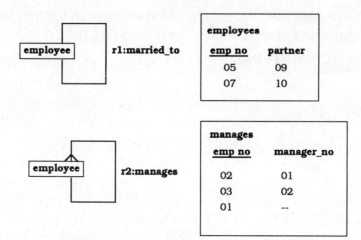

Figure 9.1

same domain as *empno*. The same applies to the one-to-many relationship *manages* in figure 9.1. *Empno* is the key; *manager_no* is defined on the same domain. The table differs from the one discussed earlier however in that whereas partner is a unique foreign key, *manager_no* is not unique. We need two tables to represent the many-to-many relationship between parts: one to record parts information, and the other to record the relationships between parts. Because we have two one-to-many relation-

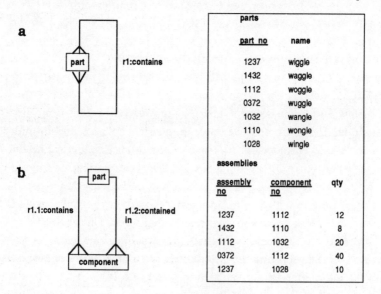

Figure 9.2

ships into the table *assemblies* we form a compound key from the two attributes defined on the same domain as *part_no*.

9.3 Roles

In the manages relationship in figure 9.1 the employee entity acts in two different ways - as a manager, and as a subordinate. These two different perspectives on the same entity are known as the entity's *roles*. An employee may act in the role of a manager in one record, and in the role of worker in another record.

Roles however are not solely of relevance to unary relationships. They are equally of relevance to binary relationships. The two distinct relationships between customers and products indicated in figure 9.3, for instance, mean that the customer entity must act in two different roles towards products. A customer is both a person who orders products, and a person who receives products.

For each role representing a one-to-many relationship we need a distinct foreign key. Hence, in the example in figure 9.3 *order_cust* and *ship_cust* are defined on the same domain as *cust_no*.

9.4 Ternary Relationships

The relationship *skill_used* in figure 9.4 associates the entities *employee*,

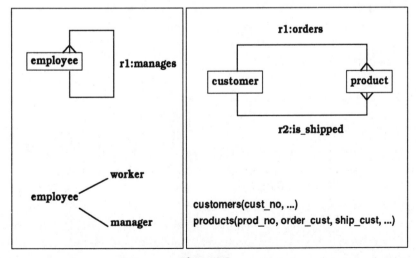

Figure 9.3

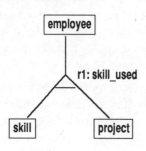

skill_used		
emp no	skill no	proj name
38	27	gamma
38	51	gamma
38	27	delta
38	03	delta

Figure 9.4

skill and *project*. Such a relationship is known as a ternary relationship.

Ternary relationships are only used when they cannot be decomposed into a series of binary relationships. Ternary relationships cannot be decomposed into binary relationships if the relation used to represent the relationship is in fourth normal form. If we attempt to fragment the relation *skill_used*, for instance, into any two relations we lose valuable information.

Since all three entities must co-exist in the same relationship we need a compound key composed of the identifiers of all participating entities.

9.5 Abstraction Mechanisms

The major problem inherent in modelling any subset of the 'real world' in a database is the distinction between a human's perception of the 'real world' and the need to organise real-world knowledge into structures for efficient storage and retrieval. A number of researchers have attempted to address this issue by proposing mechanisms closer to those which appear to be used by human beings when confronted by large amounts of data. These are the so-called abstraction mechanisms.

A number of abstraction mechanisms have been proposed for database design. Three fundamental abstraction mechanisms have been found important for such work: generalisation, aggregation and association.

Perhaps the most popular abstraction mechanism is that of generalisation. Generalisation is the process by which a higher-order entity is formed by emphasising the similarities between a number of lower-level entities. An *employee* entity, for instance, might be considered a generalisation of *manager*, *secretary*, *technician* etc. A *publication* entity might likewise be considered a generalisation of *book, journal, magazine* etc. One way of indicating generalisation is by nesting lower-order entity boxes within higher-order entity boxes (Harel, 1986). Higher order entities are frequently referred to as classes, while lower-order entities are referred to as sub-classes or sub-types (see figure 9.5).

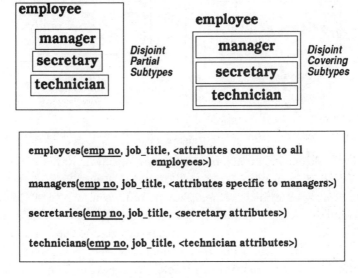

Figure 9.5

It is useful to make a distinction between partial and covering subtypes of an entity. If subtypes are partial then other subtypes can be included. If subtypes are covering then no further subtypes are permitted. Hence, if we regard *manager, secretary* and *technician* as partial subtypes of an employee then other subtypes such as *shop-floor worker* are possible. If these are covering subtypes then *manager, secretary* and *technician* are the only types of employee we can have in our company.

The lower-order entities in the two examples given above probably do not overlap. A *manager* cannot be a *secretary* or a *technician,* and a *book* cannot be a *journal* or a *magazine.* We can conceive of real-world situations however where the concepts embodied in entity-types do overlap. Hence we might define two types of *computing_professional* - *systems analyst* and *programmer* - which in many firms frequently do overlap. In such cases we draw overlapping boxes (see figure 9.6).

Generalisation can be mapped onto the relational model in a number of ways. One method is to create a table for each of the lower-level entities, and a table for the higher-level or generic entity. One identifier such as

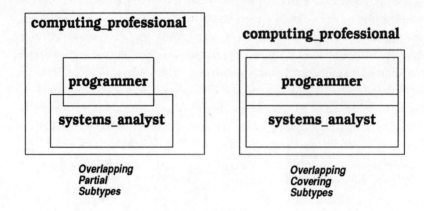

Figure 9.6

employee_no is used in all tables to identify specific instances of both the generic and the lower-level entities. We then partition different types of the generic entity in terms of values of an attribute common to all the lower-level entities. In the example in figure 9.5, *job_type* is a suitable choice.

Aggregation and association can also be represented on E-R diagrams. Aggregation is the process by which a higher-level object is used to group together a number of lower-level objects. For instance, *ISBN, title, author, publisher* and *date of publication* may all be aggregated together to form a book entity. In the E-R model, therefore, aggregation is implicit in assigning attributes to an entity. Association is a form of abstraction in which instances of one object are associated with instances of another object. Association is, of course, implicit in the way we define relationships on entity models.

9.6 Levelling

As a general rule we might state:

> *The usefulness of any Entity-Relationship diagram is inversely proportional to the size of the entity model depicted.*

This means that large diagrams spread over very large pieces of paper and containing many entities and relationships are difficult to understand, present, maintain, and reproduce. A number of people have therefore proposed that E-R diagrams should be levelled in much the same way that data flow diagrams are levelled (Beynon-Davies, 1989). In other words, we should build a hierarchy of successively more detailed E-R diagrams. At the top-most level we conceive of a corporation as being made up of a number of higher-level entities. A number of these higher-level entities may then be 'exploded' into more detail on a subject-level E-R diagram. At the lowest level of the hierarchy, the information level, we maintain E-R diagrams in the conventional sense. These form the terminal nodes of our hierarchy and are composed of explosions of entities at the subject level. Figure 9.7 illustrates the process of forming a levelled set of Entity-Relationship diagrams. Figure 9.8 illustrates a levelled segment of part of some company's global data model.

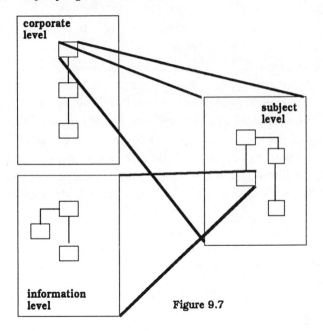

Figure 9.7

Rather than conducting a top-down levelling of diagrams, an alternative approach has been suggested. Here we attempt a bottom-up clustering of already existing entity models into higher levels of abstraction. For a discussion of this approach readers are referred to Teorey (1990).

9.7 An Extended Entity-Relationship Diagram

Figure 9.9 illustrates how all the concepts so far discussed in this chapter can be put together in one diagram. *Personnel unit* is a higher level or-

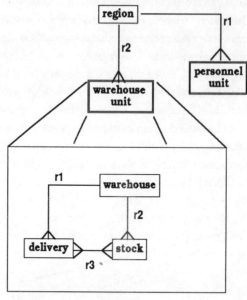

Figure 9.8

ganising entity in our data model. It acts, if you like, as a container for the entities and relationships expressed in the exploded area of the figure. *Skill, project unit* and *employee* form a ternary relationship. *Project unit* is a levelled entity in turn which probably will be exploded elsewhere in our

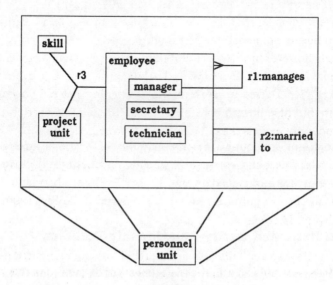

Figure 9.9

documentation. *Employee* is a generalisation of the *manager, secretary,* and *technician* entities. *Employee* is also in two recursive relationships with itself. An *employee* can be married to another *employee*. A manager employee manages numerous other employees.

9.8 Entities to Objects

In recent years great interest has been expressed in the idea of object-orientation. This idea, which originated in the development of object-oriented programming languages, has begun to mature in the development of object-oriented DBMS and is beginning to migrate into object-oriented analysis and design (Beynon-Davies, 1991a).

It is fortunate that entity modelling as we have described it in this chapter has much in common with object modelling (Blaha et al, 1988). In this section we consider some of the common threads between entity and object modelling and discuss briefly some proposals for extending entity modelling into an object modelling approach.

In chapter 6 we defined an entity as being something of interest to an organisation which has an independent existence. This abstract definition can serve equally well for defining objects. The major difference between entities and objects lies in the way we apply these constructs in the modelling process. Entities are primarily static constructs. An entity model gives us a useful framework for painting the structural detail of a database sytem. An entity model translates into files and relationships between files in some database system.

Objects however have a more ambitious purpose. An object is designed to encapsulate both a structural and behavioural aspect. In other words, an object model gives us a means for designing not only a database structure but also how that database structure is to be used. An object model not only models files, it also models transactions.

The easiest way to begin to build an object model is to exploit some of the inherent strengths of entity modelling and extend them with some behavioural abstractions.

9.9 Object Models

In this section we shall discuss an approach to object-oriented analysis and design based on a method proposed by Coad and Yourdon (1990). This methodology builds directly on some of the extensions to entity modelling discussed in this chapter.

An object is a package of data and procedures. Data are contained in attributes of an object. Procedures are defined by an object's methods. In the Coad and Yourdon approach objects are drawn as rounded boxes with a tripartite division. In the top-most division we place the object's name. In the middle division we place attributes of the object. In the bottom-most division we place the methods defined for the object. Figure 9.10 illustrates a simple object defined in this manner.

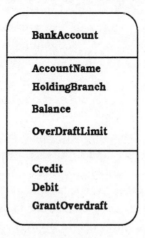

Figure 9.10

In the same way that we distinguished between entities and entity types we should strictly distinguish between an object and an object class. An object class is a grouping of similar objects that define their attributes and methods. Objects are instances of some class. They have the same attributes and methods. Hence, figure 9.10 truly illustrates an object class. Two objects of this class are illustrated in figure 9.11. In other words, object classes define the intension of the database - the central topic of database design. Objects define the extension of a database - the central topic of database implementation.

We have defined three methods for the object class in figure 9.10: Credit, Debit and GrantOverdraft. Methods provide the link between data and transactions. In a truly object-oriented manner transactions impact upon data (attributes) through messages. Credits and debits, for instance, are messages which activate the methods of the object class and update the balance attributes of object instances.

Methods may also be used to incorporate integrity constraints. Hence

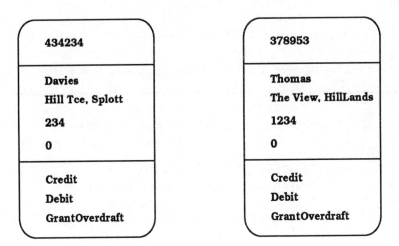

Figure 9.11

the GrantOverdraft method might incorporate a check on a person's credit-worthiness. This would mean sending a message to another object and receiving some reply. Figure 9.12 illustrates a message dependency (indicated by the arrow) between a customer class and a bankaccount class. Figure 9.13 illustrates how we might use a formal specifiation language to define each of the objects in our application. Note how we have used a production rule-like syntax to specify methods (Blaha et al, 1988).

Transactions can be modelled using methods. Most objects relevant to database systems will have the following standard methods declared in the specifications of classes: CreateInstance, DeleteInstance, AmendInstance and RetrieveInstance. In relational terms these methods will be

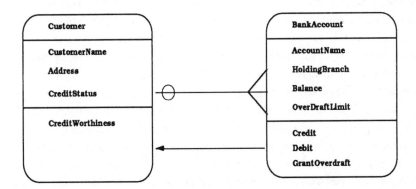

Figure 9.12

DEFINE Customer CLASS
ATTRIBUTES:
CustomerName
Address
CreditStatus
METHOD: CreditWorthiness
IF CreditStatus IS 'good'
THEN CreditWorthiness IS 'sound'
END

DEFINE BankAccount CLASS
ATTRIBUTES:
AccountName
HoldingBranch
Balance
OverdraftLimit
METHOD: GrantOverdraft
IF CreditWorthiness IS 'sound' THEN
OverDraftLimit = 500
METHOD: Credit
Balance = Balance + Amount
METHOD: Debit
Balance = Balance - Amount
END

Figure 9.13

taken as specifications of generic SQL insert, update, delete and select statements.

Any given specification for a method may also contain within it a definition of the static and/or transition constraints that might apply. For instance, in the DeleteInstance method associated with the customer object class we might include what amounts to a restricted delete constraint. We prohibit the deletion of an instance of customer until all associated bankaccount instances have been deleted.

Figure 9.14 documents a slightly more involved object model. Here we have a simple generalisation hierarchy between two distinct types of insurance policy. Generalisation is indicated in this notation by a semi-circle on the junction of relationship lines. Figure 9.15 indicates how we might specify the objects. Note how the HandleClaim method is specified differently in the two sub-classes of insurance policy.

Object-oriented analysis and design has been seen by many as an important step forward in integrating data-directed methods such as entity modelling with process-directed such as data flow diagramming (Yourdon, 1990). Unlike object-oriented programming however, which is a relatively well-developed technology, object-oriented analysis and design is still in its infancy.

9.10 Conclusion

In this chapter we have considered the following extensions to the

An insurance policy is identified by a unique policy number, and requires payment of a premium. Policies are either for life insurance, in which case the age of the insured life is recorded, or for vehicle insurance, in which case a 'no claims' bonus may have been earned.

If a claim is made against a vehicle policy then the no claims bonus is nullified. If a claim is made against a life policy then the policy is deleted.

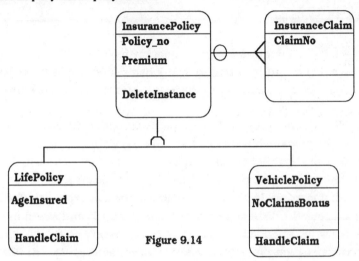

Figure 9.14

fundamentals of the entity-relationship approach as discussed in chapters 6 and 7: recursive relationships; roles; ternary relationships; generalisation; levelling; object modelling.

DEFINE InsurancePolicy CLASS
ATTRIBUTES:
PolicyNo
Premium
SET OF InsuranceClaim
METHOD: DeleteInstance
DELETE OBJECT of CLASS WITH IDENTITY PolicyNo
END

DEFINE InsurancePolicy CLASS
ATTRIBUTES:
ClaimDate
END

DEFINE VehiclePolicy SUBCLASS of insurancePolicy
ATTRIBUTES:
NoClaimsBonus
METHOD: HandleClaim
IF InsuranceClaim IS 'valid'
THEN NoClaimsBonus = NULL
END

DEFINE LifePolicy SUBCLASS of InsurancePolicy
ATTRIBUTES:
AgeInsured
METHOD: HandleClaim
DeleteInstance
END

Figure 9.15

Many attempts have been made to build a coherent methodology for applying these extended constructs. A good example is the work by Teorey et al (1986).

9.11 Exercises

(1) What is meant by a recursive relationship?

(2) What is meant by a ternary relationship, and why is it needed?

(3) Describe what is meant by the term role in the context of entities and relationships.

(4) What do you think might be appropriate optionalities for the entities in the relationships in figures 9.1 and 9.2?

(5) Why are abstraction mechanisms important for database design?

(6) How might views be used to handle generalisation?

(7) What is meant by the term levelling in the context of E-R diagrams?

(8) Discuss the distinction between entity models and object models.

(9) Draw an extended E-R diagram to represent the following animal classification problem: Lions and Tigers are big cats; Big Cats are Mammals; Mammals are Animals.

Chapter 10
View Integration

10.1 Introduction

In chapters 6 and 7 we discussed the process of building a single entity model for an application. The process described is a simplification of the process of entity modelling. In building any reasonably large entity model there will usually be a number of different viewpoints on the given application. Each distinct viewpoint will generate a different entity model. These differing perspectives are frequently referred to as user views.

Since the present generation of DBMS can handle only one database schema, differing perspectives on a given application have to be reconciled in some way. This is what is meant by the process of view integration.

View integration however may not simply be about reconciling different perspectives. It also encompasses the situation in which a jigsaw puzzle has to be assembled from separate pieces. For a large database application designing a system may be too complex a task to be undertaken in one go, or undertaken by one person. The database design will have to be built up from a series of smaller design activities, probably undertaken by a team of data analysts (see figure 10.1).

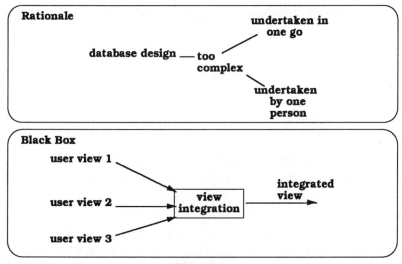

Figure 10.1

View integration is a topic that deserves a work in its own right. In this chapter we merely introduce some of the principles involved. Readers wishing to know more about the process are referred to Batini et al (1986).

10.2 Differences in Views

Figures 10.2 and 10.3 introduce some of the ways in which two or more entity models drawn from the same universe of discourse may be different.

Probably the most commonplace difference arises when the same real-world entity is named differently in two or more entity models. In figure 10.2a, for instance, a *client* and a *customer* are held to be synonyms for the same real-world entity.

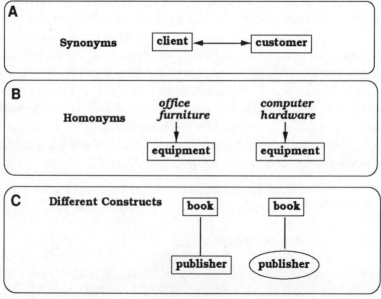

Figure 10.2

In contrast, figure 10.2b illustrates the situation where the same label is used in two or more entity models, but the label actually describes two distinct real-world entities. In figure 10.2b *equipment* is a homonym. It is used to refer both to the office furniture sold by a given company, and to the company's computer hardware.

Because of the inherent flexibility of the approach a given real-world situation can be represented in more than one way using the constructs of E-R diagramming. In figure 10.2c, for example, *publisher* might be documented as an entity or an attribute. One user sees publishers as important things of interest, another user sees them to be of lesser importance.

There is scope within any modelling technique for making errors. The advantage of a graphic technique such as E-R diagramming is that these errors are made more explicit. Figure 10.3a, for instance, illustrates the situation in which one data analyst has represented the relationship between employees and projects as a one-to-one relationship. The actual situation is represented by the data analyst documenting a many-to-many relationship.

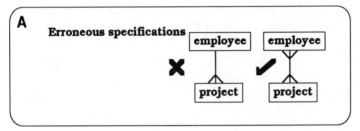

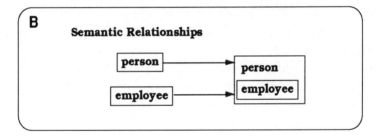

Figure 10.3

Some relationships between entities in a given entity model may however be more implicit rather than explicit. Take the situation illustrated in figure 10.3b. *Person* and *employee* are represented on the original entity model as seperate entities. In fact, *person* could be regarded as a super-class of *employee*. There is therefore certainly some scope for amalgamation.

10.3 A Study in View Integration

Let us now illustrate how some of these techniques are applicable within a small exercise in view integration.

Two entity models are illustrated in figure 10.4. Both entity models represent attempts at documenting the same application - book publish-

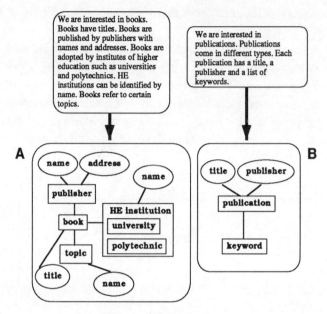

Figure 10.4

ing. Each model however has been derived from a separate requirements analysis. The boxed text in figure 10.4 is meant to summarise some of the differences in these initial requirements. Entity model A is clearly derived from a more detailed set of requirements than entity model B.

In the sections that follow we shall illustrate how a consensus representation might be achieved from elements of both entity models. This two-way integration is meant solely to illustrate the process of integrating multiple views. Some research has been conducted into automating the process of integration. The reader is referred to Navathe et al (1986) and Storey and Goldstein (1988).

10.4 Identifying Synonyms

The first logical step we might take is to attempt to identify synonyms in the two entity models. Examining each entity in turn we find that the *keyword* entity in model B is a synonym for the *topic* entity in A. Finding topic to be a more general label than keyword we choose to rename the entity in B *topic* (see figure 10.5).

Note that in the process of identifying synonyms we would also be checking for homonyms. We would ask ourselves questions like: *is title the same attribute in A as it is in B?* In this integration exercise we happen to

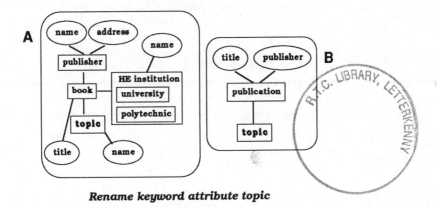

Rename keyword attribute topic

Figure 10.5

answer in the affirmative. In another exercise we might choose to distinguish between these two constructs by applying distinguishing labels.

10.5 Merging Different Constructs

The next step we take is to merge elements in our entity models that are currently represented by different E-R constructs (see figure 10.6). Consider, for example, the *publisher* attribute in B. Because we consider information about publishers to be of fundamental importance to the book business we feel that it should be promoted to the status of an entity. This brings it into line with the construction of entity model A. Note also how

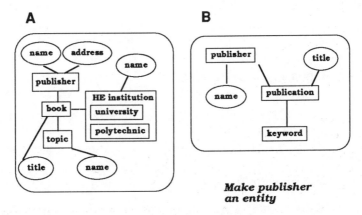

*Make publisher
an entity*

Figure 10.6

in transforming *publisher* to an entity we connect the attribute name to the new entity.

10.6 Superimposing Diagrams

We are now in a position to superimpose one diagram upon the other. This gives us the composite diagram in figure 10.7. All the relationships in the original entity models are present in the single composite diagram.

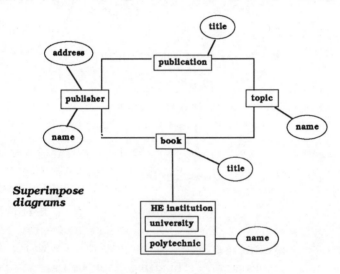

Figure 10.7

10.7 Simplifying Diagrams

In drawing any diagram we are always looking for means of simplification. One useful technique in this respect is the abstraction mechanism of generalisation as discussed in section 9.5.

Figure 10.8 illustrates a modified entity model in which we have proposed a new organisation for *publication* and *book*. *Publication* is indicated here as a class entity. *Book* is regarded as one instance of this class. Other types of publication are *journals, conference proceedings* etc.

10.8 Methods for View Integration

A number of methodologies have been proposed for conducting view integration. Any such methodology however can be considered as a mix of

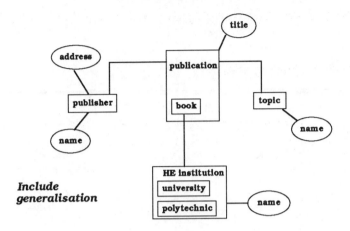

Figure 10.8

the following activities:

(1) Pre-integration. An analysis of views is carried out prior to integration to determine a policy for integration. Such a policy governs the choice of views to be integrated, the order of integration and a possible assignment of priorities to entire views or parts of views. Giving preference to financial applications over production applications is an example of a policy for integration assigned by management.

For all methodologies the sequencing and grouping of views for integration has to be considered in this phase. Batini et al (1986), discuss two major strategies for integration processing:

(a) Binary strategies allow the integration only of two views at a time. These break down into the following sub-types:

(i) Ladder strategies are those in which a new component view is integrated with an intermediate result at each step.

(ii) Balanced strategies are those in which the views are divided into pairs and integrated in a symmetric fashion.

(b) N-ary strategies allow the integration of n component views at a time (n > 2).

(i) An n-ary strategy is one-shot when n schemas are integrated in a single step.

(ii) An n-ary strategy is iterative when a number of steps are needed to arrive at an integrated view.

These strategies are illustrated in figure 10.9.

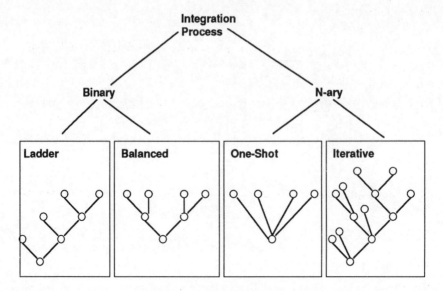

Figure 10.9

(2) Comparison of Views. Views are analysed and compared to detect both correspondences between views and possible areas of conflict.

(3) Conforming the Views. Once conflicts are detected, an effort is made to resolve them so that merging of various views becomes possible. This must be achieved by close interaction between designers and users. The intention is to arrive at some compromise.

(4) Merging and Restructuring the Views. Views are superimposed, giving rise to some intermediate integrated view. The process continues until all component views are integrated. At each step integrated views are analysed in terms of four important properties:

    (a) Completeness. The integrated view must be a representation of the union of the application domains represented by the views.

    (b) Correctness. The integrated view must contain all concepts present in each component view and represent them correctly.

    (c) Minimality. If the same concept is represented in more than one component view, then it must be represented only once in the integrated schema.

    (d) Understandability. Assessing the several possible results of integration in terms of which is the easiest to understand both by the end-user and the designer

10.9 Conclusion

The current body of work addressing the view integration problem divides itself into two main streams:

(1) Those that use the relational model or extended relational model directly.
(2) Those that use semantic data models; the E-R model and its variants being the most dominant.

View modelling and view integration introduce an attractive degree of flexibility into the technique of entity modelling. It is useful in that they encourage designers to document differing organisational perspectives in terms of differing entity models. View integration is therefore a useful exercise in the pragmatics of information systems. We return to this issue of pragmatics in chapter 14.

10.10 Exercises

(1) Discuss the distinction between view modelling and view integration?
(2) Why is view integration important to database design?
(3) Name three common differences between user views.
(4) How is generalisation applicable to view integration?
(5) Why do many authors propose a pre-integration phase?

Chapter 11
Criminal Court Cases:
A Case Study in Design

11.1 Introduction

In this chapter we shall consider how the two major approaches of logical database design interact in terms of one case study: the scheduling of criminal court cases. Our objective is to illustrate how practical database design is frequently a compromise between the results suggested by a top-down approach, and the results proposed by a bottom-up approach - this we shall refer to as the process of reconciliation. Where relevant we shall also discuss the place of view modelling and view integration.

11.2 The Top-Down Approach

To perform data analysis in a top-down manner we need to have conducted some preliminary elicitation of the rules applying to a particular business. These business rules constitute a series of assertions about our universe of discourse - in this case, relationships between things of interest to the scheduling of criminal court cases. A number of assertions for this particular real-world domain are listed in figure 11.1.

Assertions	Business Rules

Each judge has a list of outstanding cases over which he will preside.

Only one judge presides per case.

For each case one prosecuting counsel is appointed to represent the Department of Public Prosecutions.

Cases are scheduled at one Crown Court for an estimated duration from a given start date.

A case can try more than one crime.

Each crime can have one or more defendants.

Each defendant can have one or more defending barristers.

If a crime has multiple defendants, each defendant can have one or more defense counsel defending.

Defendants may have more than one outstanding case against them.

Figure 11.1

The next step is to document these assertions in an Entity-Relationship diagram. Thus we identify entities and relationships and highlight the degrees and optionality associated with each relationship. Figure 11.2 illustrates an E-R diagram of this form. Note that we have chosen to make *court, duration* and *start_date* attributes of the *case* entity. We could have made these entities in themselves, but have chosen to give them a lesser role because of their use in defining the characteristics of the *case* entity. Note also that one assertion in figure 11.1 refers to a *defending barrister* while another assertion refers to a *defence counsel*. Defence counsel and defence barristers are synonymous. We have therefore chosen to refer to this entity by the label *defence counsel*. This is an example of the merging of constructs as discussed in chapter 10.

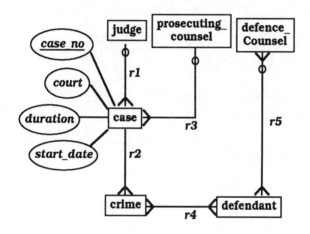

Figure 11.2

Frequently, it is not possible to fully complete an E-R diagram from the available business rules. A draft E-R diagram however is useful in highlighting gaps in our knowledge of some application. The most common area for this to arise is in identifying appropriate optionalities. The reader will note that there is little in the business rules to tell us whether, for instance, *defence counsel* in the relationship *r5* is optional or mandatory. This is one of the major reasons we choose to document business rules in a diagram. An E-R diagram immediately highlights areas that demand further elicitation. Note that in our application further elicitation has identified *judge, prosecuting counsel,* and *defence counsel* as optional in their associated relationships.

11.3 The Data Dictionary

An E-R diagram is insufficient in itself to fully document all we need to know of an entity model for some application. With any realistic application the E-R diagram should be supplemented with a corresponding logical data dictionary. As a bare minimum we need to document as unambiguously as possible what we mean by each of the entities on the diagram. In our notation, we have chosen to refer to relationships merely by references such as *r1*. In our data dictionary therefore we need to describe in more detail the actual semantics underlying each relationship. Figures 11.3 and 11.4 show some simple formats for documenting entities and relationships as discussed in the chapter on data dictionaries.

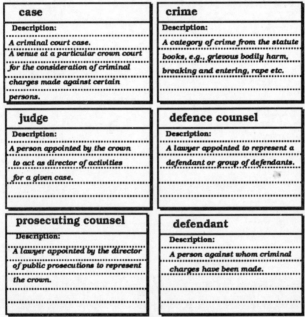

case
Description:
A criminal court case.
A venue at a particular crown court for the consideration of criminal charges made against certain persons.

crime
Description:
A category of crime from the statute books, e.g. grievous bodily harm, breaking and entering, rape etc.

judge
Description:
A person appointed by the crown to act as director of activities for a given case.

defence counsel
Description:
A lawyer appointed to represent a defendant or group of defendants.

prosecuting counsel
Description:
A lawyer appointed by the director of public prosecutions to represent the crown.

defendant
Description:
A person against whom criminal charges have been made.

Figure 11.3

A major objective of drawing E-R diagrams is to aim for simplicity. This normally means attempting to keep the number of constructs on an E-R diagram to a minimum. One of the ways we can do this in terms of our sample application, is to combine the *defence counsel* entity with the *prosecuting counsel* entity in one to be renamed simply *counsel*.

The reason for doing this is that the *prosecuting counsel* entity and the *defence counsel* entity actually represent a single real-world concept - that of a lawyer. This means that the information we would like to store about *prosecuting counsel* and *defence counsel* is likely to be the same. Only the

r1	**r2**
Name: *presides*	Name: *contains*
Entity1: *judge* Entity2: *case*	Entity1:*case* Entity2:*crime*
Degree: *1* Degree: *M*	Degree: *1* Degree: *M*
Optionality: *O* Optionality:	Optionality: Optionality:
Description: *One judge sits on each case.*	Description:*Each case can try many types of crime.*

r3	**r4**
Name: *prosecutes*	Name: *charged_with*
Entity1:*prosecuting counsel* Entity2: *case*	Entity1: *crime* Entity2: *defendant*
Degree: *1* Degree: *M*	Degree: *M* Degree: *M*
Optionality: *O* Optionality:	Optionality: Optionality:
Description: *One prosecutor is appointed per case.*	Description:*Types of crime against defendants.*

r5
Name: *defends*
Entity1:*defence counsel* Entity2: *defendant*
Degree: *M*   Degree: *M*
Optionality: *O*   Optionality:
Description: *at least one defence counsel per defendant.*

Figure 11.4

roles that individual instances of our counsel entity play are likely to be different. Although most lawyers specialise, it is perfectly feasible for a given lawyer to be a prosecutor at one time and a defence lawyer at another. Figure 11.5 documents this change which is really a variant of a view integration strategy discussed in chapter 10.

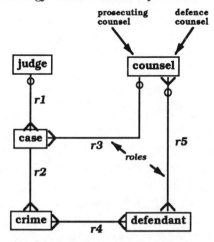

Figure 11.5

Figure 11.6 illustrates how we might break down the many-to-many relationships on our diagram into one-to-many relationships. The major reason for doing this is to simplify the accommodation to a relational schema. The intermediate entity, *criminal offence*, is now made up of instances of specific crimes committed by specific persons. The intermediate entity, *defence*, is made up of instances of specific counsel defending specific defendants.

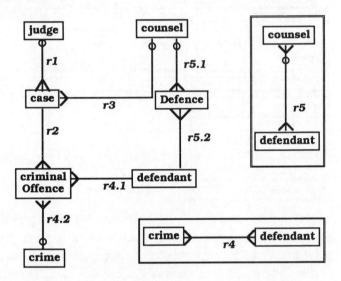

Figure 11.6

Note how in the new diagram, our numbering convention indicates the existence of many-to-many breakdowns. The relationships *r5.1* and *r5.2* are easily identified as the breakdown of a many-to-many relationship *r5*.

Creating table structures from the diagram in figure 11.6 is a relatively straightforward process. For each entity on our diagram we create a table. It is conventional to take the name of the entity and make it a plural wherever possible to form the table name. Hence *judge* becomes the table *judges* and *defendant* becomes the table *defendants*.

If our analysis of the application has not already provided this for us, we think up suitable identifiers for each of the entities. A non-mnemonic serial number, such as a judge number, is usually the best choice. The last step is to post identifiers from the table representing the one end of a relationship into the table representing the many end of a relationship. Hence, for instance, we post *judge_no* from the *judges* table into the *cases* table. The complete relational schema is presented as follows:

Judges(judge_no, ...)
Cases(case_no, judge_no, counsel_no, court, start_date, duration, ...)
Counsel(counsel_no, ...)
Offences(offence_no, case_no, defendant_no, crime_no, ...)
Defendants(defendant_no, ...)
Defence(defendant_no, counsel_no, ...)
Crimes(crime_no, ...)

11.4 The Bottom-Up Approach

In contrast to the top-down approach where we work at a high-level with 'things of interest', to conduct a data analysis exercise in a bottom-up manner we need a sample data-set in place. Let us suppose therefore that we have examined the manual documentation existing in the present criminal court case system and produced the sample data-set below:

Judge No.	Judge Name	Case No.	Start Date	Court	Def. No.	Def. Name	Crime	Def. Counsel	Pros. Counsel
01	Farmer	569	01/09/89	C1	2456	I.Vaughan	Car Theft	Davies	Smythe
02	Jennings	325	01/09/89	C2	2457	T.Smith	Burglary	Evans	Raleigh
02	Jennings	325	01/09/89	C2	2459	C.Burgh	Burglary	Beynon	Raleigh
01	Farmer	576	21/02/90	C2	3001	R.Davy	Rape	Beynon	Smythe
03	Gordon	603	21/09/89	S1	3012	G.Basle	GBH	Evans	Raleigh
03	Gordon	603	21/09/89	S1	3013	T.Evans	GBH	Evans	Raleigh
03	Gordon	666	01/11/89	S2	3056	R.Thomas	Fraud	Evans	Raleigh
03	Gordon	890	01/01/90	S2	3111	I.Blythe	Exposure	Davies	Smythe
02	Jennings	9000	01/01/90	C1	4021	T.Johns	Fraud	Beynon	Smythe

Our task is now to identify dependencies between data items in the table. Hence, for instance, there is a clear functional dependency between *judge_no* and *judge_name*. Whenever a given *judge_no* appears such as *02,* a given *judge_name* is always associated with it, such as *Jennings.*

Figure 11.7 documents all the dependencies identified from the unnormalised table above. Note that they appear to be all functional dependencies.

To accommodate a determinancy diagram to a relational schema it is useful to draw boundaries around the data items which will be used to

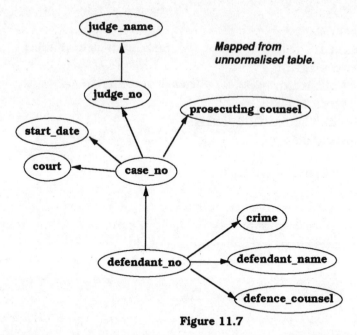

Figure 11.7

form tables. This means drawing a boundary around each determinant and its immediate dependants. Figure 11.8 illustrates the appropriate boundaries for the diagram in figure 11.7.

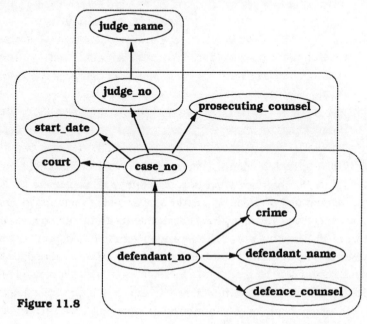

Figure 11.8

Having done this, the process of forming table-structures is straightforward. Each determinant becomes the primary key of a table. All immediate dependent data items are placed in the table. Since we have three determinants in our diagram we end up with three tables. Note how foreign keys arise out of dependent data items which are themselves determinants.

Judges(judge no, judge_name, ...)

Cases(case no, judge_no, prosecuting_counsel, court, start_date, ...)

Defendants(defendant no, defendant_name, defence_counsel, crime, case_no ...)

11.5 The Process of Reconciliation

The reader will note that the tables arising from our bottom-up analysis do not match with the tables constructed from our top-down data analysis. Three tables are produced bottom-up, compared with seven tables produced top-down.

If we compare the information documented on our E-R diagram with the information documented on our determinancy diagram, a number of key differences can be identified:

(1) Our determinancy diagram proposes fundamentally a one-to-many relationship between *defendant* and *crime* via a functional dependency between *defendant_no* and *crime_no*. The E-R diagram documents this as a many-to-many relationship.

(2) The same is true for *defendant* and *defence counsel*. The determinancy diagram models this as a one-to-many relationship via a functional dependency from *defendant_no* to *defence_counsel*,; the E-R diagram models it as a many-to-many relationship.

This discrepancy should force us to re-evaluate the knowledge elicited for our E-R diagram, determinancy diagram, or both. Let us suppose that we find in discussions with our users that our E-R diagram is the most accurate representation. This would mean that we would need to redraft our determinancy diagram into a form similar to that illustrated in figure 11.9.

The many-to-many relationship between *defendant* and *defence*

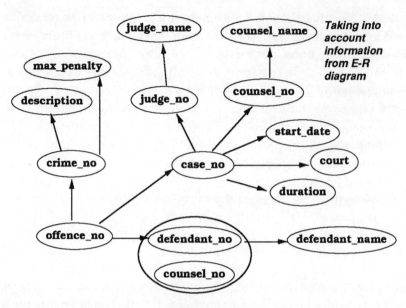

Figure 11.9

counsel is represented on the new determinancy diagram by a multi-valued dependency between *defendant_no* and *counsel_no*. The many-to-many relationship between *defendant* and *crime* is represented by inter-posing the data item *offence_no* between *defendant_no* and *crime_no*.

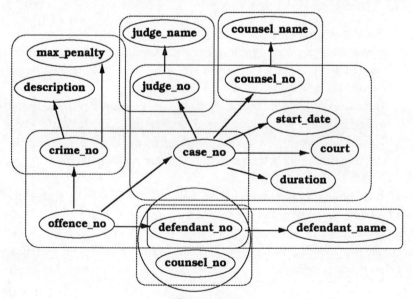

Figure 11.10

Drawing boundaries around data-items as in figure 11.10 means we need to revise our relational schema such that we arrive at the following set of table structures.

Judges(<u>judge no</u>, judge_name, ...)
Cases(<u>case no</u>, judge_no, counsel_no, court, start_date, duration, ...)
Counsel(<u>counsel no</u>, counsel_name, ...)
Offences(<u>offence no</u>, case_no, defendant_no, crime_no, ...)
Defendants(<u>defendant no</u>, defendant_name, ...)
Defence(<u>defendant no, counsel no</u>, ...)
Crimes(<u>crime no</u>, description, max_penalty, ...)

11.6 Conclusion

In this chapter we have considered how the process of practical data analysis is a process of reconciliation. The end-result of the data analysis exercise - a logical database design expressed as a set of table structures - is a compromise between the results of a top-down approach, and the results of a bottom-up approach (see figure 11.11). The approach taken in most database development projects is usually to concentrate on a top-

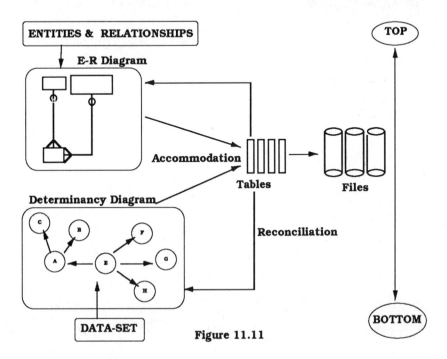

Figure 11.11

down approach and use a bottom-up approach primarily as a means of validating subsets of the developing conceptual model. This is because the number of attributes generated by a realistic application is generally too large to handle in one normalisation exercise.

In this chapter we have discussed a simple iteration between these two complementary design techniques. We have merely iterated once from E-R diagram to determinancy diagram to E-R diagram and back to determinancy diagram. In practice, the iteration is more frequent and more complex than that discussed. Also, the iteration is used much more consciously as a direction for further elicitation.

This is, of course, not the end of the story. Data analysis, whether by bottom-up or top-down means, only provides a logical model of our application. The next step is to translate the logical model into a physical model. That is, a schema expressed in the syntax of the data definition language of some RDBMS. It is to this topic that we now turn.

11.7 Exercises

(1) Document the dependency diagram in figure 11.9 as a set of data dictionary structures.
(2) Annotate the final relational schema arrived at with foreign key indicators.
(3) Outline three queries we might commonly wish to run on this data model.

Chapter 12
Physical Database Design:
Volume and Usage Analysis

12.1 Introduction

Logical database design is the process of constructing a business data model, that is, a model of the business rules applying to some enterprise. Physical database design involves taking the results from the logical design process, fine-tuning them against the performance and storage requirements of some application and then implementing them in the mechanisms of some DBMS.

With the rise of the relational data model the emphasis has changed in the database literature. Prior to the relational data model the emphasis in texts on database design tended to concentrate on physical database design. Nowadays, the emphasis is clearly directed at logical database design. This is primarily because some success has been achieved in formalising logical design. Physical design, in comparison, is relatively unformalised. This is because the natures of the two exercises are clearly different. Logical design is about implementation independence. This makes a general analysis of the area feasible. Physical design in comparison is about implementation dependence. You cannot conduct a physical design exercise unless you know in some detail how your application is meant to work, on what hardware the application is to run, and what facilities are provided by your chosen DBMS. In this type of environment few generalities are possible.

Nevertheless, physical database design is still of extreme importance to designers and indeed users of relational database systems. This chapter, and the next, therefore provides an overview of some of the most important aspects of the physical design of relational databases.

12.2 Inputs to and Outputs from Physical Design

Figure 12.1 summarises some of the main inputs to and outputs from physical design. The main inputs are:

(1) A logical design expressed as table structures.

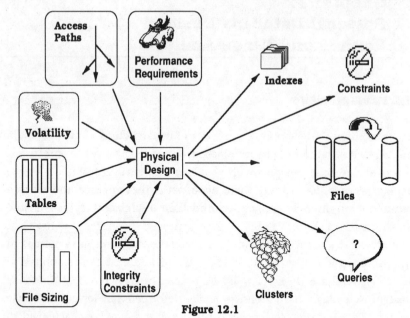

Figure 12.1

(2) A clear statement of what we mean by performance in terms of our particular application.

(3) Some estimates of how many records our files will be expected to hold.

(4) Some assessment of file usage in terms of the profile and frequency of transactions likely to impact on each file in our database.

(5) A list of integrity constraints we wish to support in our application.

(6) A list of the most frequent packaged reports to be run on our database.

The main outputs from physical design are:

(1) File structures declared in a suitable Data Definition Language (DDL).

(2) Appropriate indexes on the file structures.

(3) Clustering of files where appropriate.

(4) A set of inherent constraints expressed in some DDL, and a set of additional integrity constraints expressed in some Data Integrity Language (DIL).

(5) A set of queries optimised for running on a particular database.

In this chapter we shall consider the input side of the equation. We shall discuss how to perform a volume and usage analysis of a logical data model. In the next chapter we shall discuss how the results of this exercise help us to select amongst a range of implementation possibilities in a given DBMS.

It must be remembered however that although we have separated inputs and outputs into discrete units for convenience here, in practice the inputs and outputs are in fact interdependent.

12.3 Indemnity Insurance Revisited

To provide a useful basis for our discussion, let us revisit the case of Indemnity Insurance which we first met in chapter 6. Figure 12.2 illustrates the main entities and relationships derived from the business

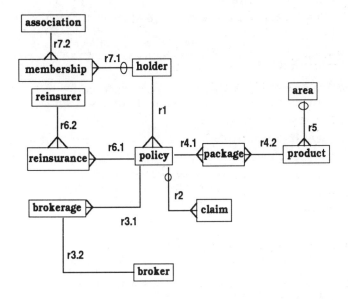

Figure 12.2

rules of Indemnity Insurance. The table structures built from the E-R diagram are outlined below as a series of create table statements expressed in ANSI SQL. Note how we have chosen suitable data types and lengths for each of the attributes. Note also how we have declared primary and foreign keys for each of the tables, and declared the null characteristics of each foreign key:

```
CREATE TABLE policies(policy_no CHAR(8) NOT NULL,
                      holder_no CHAR(8) NOT NULL,
                      renewal_date DATE NOT NULL,
                      start_yr DATE NOT NULL,
                      premium NUMBER(7,2))
PRIMARY KEY(policy_no)
FOREIGN KEY(holder_no IDENTIFIES holders)

CREATE TABLE holders(holder_no CHAR(8) NOT NULL,
                     holder_name CHAR(20) NOT NULL,
                     holder_address CHAR(50) ,
                     holder_tel_no CHAR(10) )
PRIMARY KEY(holder_no)

CREATE TABLE claims(claim_no NUMBER(8) NOT NULL,
                    policy_no CHAR(8) NOT NULL,
                    claim_type CHAR(2) NOT NULL,
                    claim_date DATE NOT NULL)
PRIMARY KEY(claim_no)
FOREIGN KEY(policy_no IDENTIFIES policies)

CREATE TABLE reinsurers(reinsurer_no CHAR(8) NOT NULL,
                        reinsurer_name CHAR(20) NOT NULL,
                        reinsurer_address CHAR(50),
                        reinsurer_tel_no CHAR(10))
PRIMARY KEY(reinsurer_no)

CREATE TABLE brokers(broker_no CHAR(8) NOT NULL,
                     broker_name CHAR(20) NOT NULL,
                     broker_address CHAR(50),
                     broker_tel_no CHAR(10))
PRIMARY KEY(broker_no)

CREATE TABLE brokerage(broker_no CHAR(8) NOT NULL,
                       policy_no CHAR(8) NOT NULL,
                       commission NUMBER(7,2),
                       payment_date DATE)
PRIMARY KEY(broker_no,policy_no)
FOREIGN KEY(policy_no IDENTIFIES policies)
FOREIGN KEY(broker_no IDENTIFIES brokers)

CREATE TABLE products(product_no CHAR(6) NOT NULL,
                      area_code CHAR(2) NOT NULL,
                      product_description CHAR(50))
PRIMARY KEY(product_no)

CREATE TABLE areas(area_code CHAR(2) NOT NULL,
                   area_description CHAR(20))
PRIMARY KEY(area_code)

CREATE TABLE associations(association_no NUMBER(6) NOT NULL,
                          association_name CHAR(20) ,
                          association_address CHAR(50),
                          association_tel_no CHAR(10))
PRIMARY KEY(association_no)
```

```
CREATE TABLE membership(association_no NUMBER(6) NOT NULL,
                        holder_no CHAR(8) NOT NULL,
                        no_of_yrs NUMBER(3))
PRIMARY KEY(association_no),holder_no)
FOREIGN KEY(holder_no IDENTIFIES holders)
FOREIGN KEY(association_no IDENTIFIES associations)

CREATE TABLE packages(policy_no NUMBER(8) NOT NULL,
                      product_no CHAR(6) NOT NULL)
PRIMARY KEY(policy_no,product_no)
FOREIGN KEY(policy_no IDENTIFIES policies)
FOREIGN KEY(product_no IDENTIFIES products)
```

12.4 What is Performance?

When relational DBMS products first emerged into the commercial arena they were heavily criticised for being poor performers. The relational data model was consequently attacked not only in its ability to support transaction-processing applications, but also in the area of decision support, where relational databases were traditionally held to be strong.

Many of these early criticisms were however mis-directed. They ignored the crucial fact that the relational data model is a logical data model. It is an abstract machine and as such is devoid of physical implementation concerns. Performance is therefore not a critical issue for the relational data model. Performance is a critical issue for relational database systems.

But what is performance? Performance is usually a balancing act. By performance do we mean access performance or update performance? Do we need a clean-cut data model amenable to change, or is our application

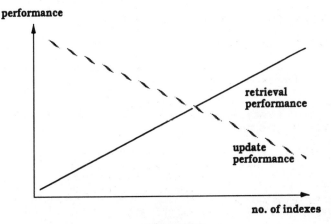

Figure 12.3

stable enough to allow the re-introduction of redundancy?

If we set fast access to data as a priority we may have to sacrifice data entry speed. By transforming your data structures to meet the needs of fast access we may have to sacrifice some aspects of a clean-cut business data model. Figure 12.3 illustrates the idea of performance as a balancing act.

The first thing any designer needs to do when conducting physical design is therefore to write a mission statement for the proposed database system. This mission statement should constitute a map of file values, usage and integrity. Throw in as many constraints as we can to be as clear as possible about what we mean by performance in terms of our particular application.

12.5 Sizing Estimates

One of the first steps we need to take in moving from logical to physical database design is to establish estimates as to the average and maximum number of instances per entity. An estimate of the maximum possible number of instances per entity is useful in deciding upon realistic storage requirements. An estimate of how many instances are likely to be present in the system on average also gives us a picture of the model's ability to fulfill access requirements. This is the topic of section 12.12. It is this problem of estimating file sizes that we consider here.

The table below summarises some provisional estimates for the Indemnity Insurance case. Using the field sizes established in the CREATE TABLE statements above it is relatively straightforward to translate entity sizing into file sizing. For each table described in our database the relevant calculations are:

Table	AVG (instances)	MAX (instances)	Record Length (characters)	File Size (characters)
Policies	500000	1000000	41	41000000
Holders	100000	500000	88	44000000
Claims	500000	750000	26	19500000
Reinsurers	500	1000	88	88000
Brokers	5000	10000	88	880000
Products	100	300	58	17400
Areas	10	30	22	660
Associations	4000	10000	86	860000
Brokerage	500000	750000	33	24750000
Membership	50000	75000	17	12750000
Packages	750000	1000000	14	14000000

12.6 Sizing Cardinality and Optionality

The reader will note two other sets of figures added to the entity model in figure 12.4. On the 'many' end of each relationship we indicate how many instances of an entity are associated on average with instances of the other entity. Hence in relationship r1 there are on average 2 policies associated with each holder.

Where optionality is relevant we indicate the estimated percentage of entities that participate in the relationship. Hence in relationship r2 80% of policies have claims made against them.

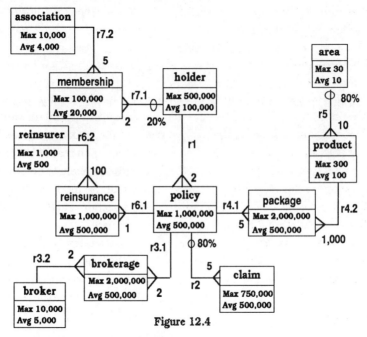

Figure 12.4

12.7 Transaction Analysis

Usage analysis requires that we identify the major transactions required against the database. Transactions are logical units of work made up of pure insertions, updates, retrievals or deletions or a mixture of all four. In section 12.12 we will consider a number of pure retrieval transactions. Below we give a sample list of insertion, update and delete transactions of relevance to Indemnity Insurance:

(1) Insert a new holder and policy made up of a package of products.

(2) Add a new claim against a policy.

(3) Purge all lapsed policies.

(4) Amend the commission paid to a broker.

(5) Record details of a holder in a particular association.

Each transaction is analysed to determine the access paths used and the estimated frequency of use. When all transactions have been analysed a composite map is prepared showing the total usage of access paths on the entity model (Martin, 1983).

Figure 12.5 shows a sample transaction analysis form. This form is being used to analyse the transaction *list claims for a given holder*. This transaction is estimated to have an average transaction volume of 2 transactions per hour and a peak volume of 10 transactions per hour. The transaction map illustrates the stages of the transaction against a subset of the Indemnity Insurance data model. The entry point is at the holder entity; then the path goes to the policy entity; then it proceeds to the claim entity.

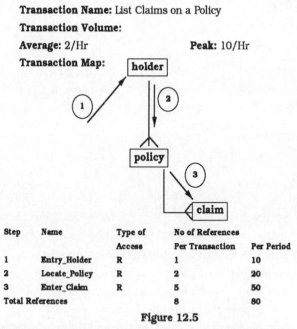

Transaction Name: List Claims on a Policy

Transaction Volume:

Average: 2/Hr   **Peak:** 10/Hr

Transaction Map:

Step	Name	Type of Access	No of References Per Transaction	Per Period
1	Entry_Holder	R	1	10
2	Locate_Policy	R	2	20
3	Enter_Claim	R	5	50
Total References			8	80

Figure 12.5

A detailed analysis of each step in the access path is entered at the bottom of the form. The type of access to each entity is recorded - R for read, I for insert, U for update and D for delete. *List_claims* requires only one holder reference per transaction. This translates to ten references per hour at peak volume. Therefore the average number of times the entry_holder path is used per transaction is 10; this translates to a peak volume of 100 transactions per hour. Finally, the entry_claim path is traversed once for each claim associated with a policy. This translates to an average volume of 20 transactions per hour and a peak volume of 200 transactions per hour. We sum the figures to give us a total of 8 references per transaction and a peak of 80 references per hour.

12.8 Composite Usage Map

When all the transactions have been analysed the transaction data is summarised on a composite usage map. The number at the head of each arrow is an estimate of the total number of references on a given access path at peak volume (see figure 12.6).

Some entities are clearly central to the application such as holder, policy and claim. Others are clearly less central such as association, reinsurer and broker. It is to the reasons for this apparent dichotomy that we now turn.

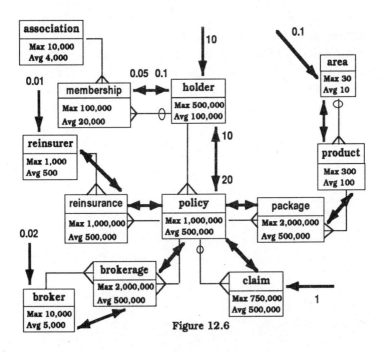

Figure 12.6

12.9 Volatility

There are two kinds of entities or files: volatile and non-volatile (Sweet, 1985). The difference between the average number of instances and maximum number of instances estimated for an entity gives us a rough idea of the volatility of an entity or file.

Imagine, for instance, a vendor file of 10,000 records. 100 new vendors are added to this file each month and 100 inactive records are purged from the file. The file's monthly volatility - turnover divided by population - is therefore 1%. Compare this with a file of purchase orders of 1,000 records, where 1,000 orders are added each month and the same number closed. The monthly volatility of this file is 100%.

If this calculation is conducted for each file in a database and the results plotted on a histogram two distinct peaks will be seen. One, centred close to 1% like vendors, and one centred close to 100% like purchase orders. Volatility appears to be a binary characteristic of files.

Let us apply this principle to the case of Indemnity Insurance. Claims is probably a volatile file. We might estimate, for instance that on average 4,000 new claims are written to this file each month and 4,000 old claims are purged from the file on average each month. The volatility of this file is clearly 100%.

The classic non-volatile file is the reference file. Areas and brokers are two files of this nature. The state of such files change relatively infrequently. Few, if any, transactions impact on these files in any one month.

As we shall see, the volatility of a file has a clear impact on its expected update and retrieval performance. We therefore mark against each of the files in the Indemnity database its expected volatility as below.

Table	Volatility
Policies	volatile
Holders	volatile
Claims	volatile
Reinsurers	non-volatile
Brokers	non-volatile
Products	non-volatile
Areas	non-volatile
Associations	volatile
Brokerage	volatile
Membership	volatile
Packages	volatile

12.10 Steady State

It is useful to visualise a database as a memory surface. We will use an analogy similar to one of De-Bono's in his book, *The Mechanism of Mind* (De-Bono, 1971). Imagine each database file as a reservoir, and the data in each file as the water in the reservoir. Insertion and update transactions correspond to water flowing into the reservoir. Deletion transactions correspond to water flowing out. This is illustrated in figure 12.7.

pooltime x flowrate = population

Figure 12.7

The amount of water in each reservoir is dependent upon two factors: pooltime and flowrate. In other words, considering any file in our database we shall find that records follow a law of steady state: the length of time that records spend in a file (pooltime), multiplied by the rate at which records flow into the file (flowrate), is numerically equal to the number of records currently in the file (population):

pooltime x flowrate = population

Steady state means that the flowrate of records into a file is equal, over a period of time, to the rate at which records leave the file. If 1,000 records are added to a file each month we would expect over a period of a year that on average 1,000 records leave the file each month.

Most database files are therefore steady state files. If more records are added each month than purged, then the file will soon outstretch its sizing. Conversely if more records are deleted each month than added then the file will soon diminish to zero.

Let us use this equation to compute the pooltime for records in one of the Indemnity files. The claims file, for example, has an average population per month of 500,000 records. We know that on average 400,000 records are written to this file every month. This gives us a pooltime of 500,000/400,000 = 1.025. The average time a record remains within the file is therefore just over one month.

12.11 The Temporal Dimension

A file's volatility is the reciprocal of its pooltime:

volatility = flowrate / population

Hence the claims file is 80% volatile. Earlier we mentioned that volatility is binary. Every file falls into one of two categories: volatile or non-volatile. The underlying reason is that in most databases we handle data representing two distinct types of real-world aspect: physical and temporal entities.

Physical entities are tangible things that exist independent of time. *Vendors, customers, products, employees, warehouses* etc. are all physical entities. The volatility of data stored about such things is low, around 1%.

Events are happenings. They have a temporal aspect. *Deliveries, shipments, orders* and *claims* are all events. Their volatility is high, around 100%.

12.12 Access Requirements

The size and volatility of a file has a clear impact on what access we can provide to data. The larger the file the more necessary it is to build access structures into the data. The more volatile the file however, the greater the penalty we pay for such access structures.

We list below six common queries or retrieval transactions to be run on the Indemnity Insurance database. These queries would be run on the database time and time again by staff at Indemnity. They therefore form suitable candidates for packaged reports.

(1) Retrieve details of all policies associated with a particular holder, giving details of products, claims and brokers.
(2) Produce a list of all holders that belong to particular associations.
(3) For each broker retrieve details of all policies and associated holders, products and claims.

(4) List all policies that have been all or part 'laid-off' with a particular reinsurer.
(5) A facility for selecting all policies due for renewal on a particular date.
(6) A facility for listing claims by claim type.

A major objective of physical database design is to ensure that the access performance of such reporting functions is satisfactory. The frequency with which each of these reports is run on the database will usually provide the database designer with sufficient information to decide upon the degree of access performance required in each case. For instance, query 1 might be run several times in every hour of every working day by members of Indemnity Insurance. Retrieval performance is therefore of the utmost importance. In contrast, query 5 is probably run once daily for a renewal date some four weeks ahead. This is to allow reminder notices to be sent out from brokers for the payments of premiums. It would therefore be sensible to run this query as an overnight batch job. Retrieval performance in this case would not be of critical importance. We list below the expected frequency of each of these reports.

(1) Retrieve details of all policies associated with a particular holder, giving details of products, claims and brokers (many per hour).
(2) Produce a list of all holders that belong to particular associations (once per quarter).
(3) For each broker retrieve details of all policies and associated holders, products and claims (once per week).
(4) List all policies that have been all or part 'laid-off' with a particular reinsurer (once per month).
(5) A facility for selecting all policies due for renewal on a particular date (once per day).
(6) A facility for listing claims by claim type (once per week).

12.13 Integrity Constraints

Classic data analysis provides us with a database design which indicates appropriate files and a set of inherent integrity constraints. Three types of inherent constraints should be documented in a relational schema:

(1) Entity integrity constraints such as *policy_no is the primary key of policies and hence that policy_no must be unique and cannot be null.*

(2) Referential integrity constraints such as *every policy must have a holders record identified by holder_no. In this business holder_no in policies cannot be null.*

(3) Domain constraints such as *the commission paid to a broker must not be greater than the premium paid on a policy.*

Additional constraints are usually needed by any application. An important class of additional constraint is the so-called transition constraint. Such constraints document valid movements from one state of the database to another. The cascades, nullifies, and restricted options associated with foreign keys are all examples of transition constraints. They indicate what should happen to records in one file when records in another associated file are inserted, updated or deleted. For example, *whenever a policy is deleted all associated claims should also be deleted,* is an example of a cascades delete.

Static constraints such as enforcing referential integrity are expensive in update performance terms. Every time a new claim record is inserted, for instance, a check will need to be made against the policies file for a valid policy_no. Transition constraints such as cascading deletes are even more expensive in update performance terms. A transaction deleting a holder record might fire off deletions in the policies file which in turn fire off deletions in the claims and packages files. One simple file maintenance operation can take a long time in these terms.

12.14 Conclusion

We began this chapter by highlighting that while generalities are possible in the area of logical database design, few such generalities are possible in the area of physical design. This is because of the inherent implementation-dependent nature of physical design.

This is particularly true of the concept of performance. Performance is a relativistic concept. It is application-specific. In conducting any physical design exercise it is therefore extremely important to construct a mission statement for the proposed application. This mission statement should contain the following items:

(1) An annotated entity model showing :
   (a) estimates of the maximum and average number of instances;

(b) numerical estimates of the cardinality and optionality associated with relationships.

(2) A set of transaction analyses and a composite usage map.

(3) Volatility percentages for each entity on the model.

(4) A list of the major integrity constraints expected for the model.

This mission statement along with the logical data model gives us a sufficient basis to make sensible decisions about implementing the application using the mechanisms available in a given DBMS. It is to this topic that we now turn.

12.15 Exercises

(1) Define Physical Design.

(2) What are the major inputs to physical design?

(3) What are the major outputs from physical design?

(4) What is the difference between update performance and retrieval performance?

(5) Define suitable file sizes for each of the criminal court cases schema defined in chapter 11.

(6) Add cardinality and optionality figures to the logical model in figure 11.3.

(7) Identify a sample of major transactions to be run on the criminal courts schema.

(8) Conduct a transaction analysis for one of these transactions.

(9) Compute a volatility percentage for each of the files in the Criminal Courts database.

(10) In computing volatility why do you think we choose flowrate into a file rather than flowrate out of a file?

(11) What sort of integrity constraints might we want on the criminal courts database?

Chapter 13
Physical Database Design:
Performance Decisions

13.1 Introduction

In the previous chapter we discussed the importance of performing a volume and usage analysis on the data model produced from logical design. This analysis can then be used to highlight areas where performance is critical to an application. In this chapter we discuss some of the major options available to the database designer in fine-tuning his application for a given DBMS. The chapter is divided into 5 major sections corresponding to the 5 major ways in which a relational database can be fine-tuned for performance:

(1) Establishing storage-related access mechanisms.
(2) Adding indexes.
(3) De-normalisation.
(4) Knowing your DBMS.
(5) Integrity Constraints.

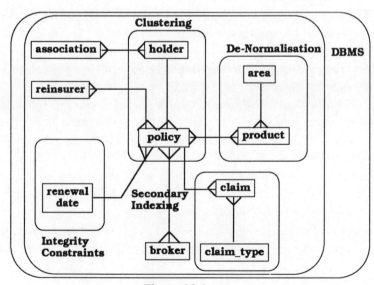

Figure 13.1

Figure 13.1 illustrates some ways in which these mechanisms apply in the Indemnity Insurance data model.

13.2 Establishing Storage-Related Access Mechanisms

In this section we discuss the three major mechanisms available in relational systems for storing data on secondary storage in a way designed for access:

(1) Sequentially.
(2) In hashed order.
(3) Clustered.

13.2.1 Sequential Scan

Every Relational Database Management System (RDBMS) offers a default mechanism for accessing data known as the sequential or relational scan. A scan is a record-by-record inspection of the rows of a table. At first sight, scans appear to be a particularly inefficient mechanism for accessing data. Scans however are recommended for:

(1) Small tables.
(2) Medium to large tables when more than 20% of rows need to be accessed to satisfy some request.
(3) Any tables which are accessed by low-priority queries or which are suitable for batch processing.

Most RDBMS scan a small table almost as fast as they access a particular row in a table.

As we shall see, for medium to large tables access performance is generally impaired by adding indexes. This is because typically Input/Output is required for the index as well as for the table. As a guideline it has been shown that a sequential scan frequently outperforms indexed access for retrievals when the hit-rate is greater than 20% of the file.

Regardless of table size, scans are almost certainly the best option for requirements that are low priority or can be run overnight.

Our volume and usage analysis should direct us to the areas within our application where sequential access is appropriate.

13.2.2 Hashing

Hashing is the process by which the DBMS converts the data values in specified columns of a table via some algorithm into a set of storage addresses for records. Hashing is conducted by defining so-called hash keys. In other words, declaring a column or series of columns on which the hashing algorithm is to be performed.

Hashing should generally be performed on medium to large tables in which:

(1) Accessing is primarily on rows in random order.
(2) The primary access method is via discrete value of the hash key in selection criteria.
(3) The hash key itself is infrequently updated.

An RDBMS can use hashing only to access rows based on a condition of the form <column name> = <hash value>.

You can only define one hash order on a table. It is therefore usual to define hashing on the primary key of a table.

Hashing conflicts with other storage-related mechanisms such as clustering. You cannot define hashing and clustering on the same table.

13.2.3 Clustering

A cluster is a set of tables which, for reasons of retrieval performance, are located contiguously on disk. Figure 13.2, for instance, illustrates a cluster of an employee table with a department table.

At first sight clustering seems to violate one of the principle tenets of the relational data model. Namely that a table should not contain duplicate rows. It must be remembered however that clustering, like indexing, is a physical implementation concern. All that matters is that end-users of the database perceive the data as being organised in tables. How the data is stored on disk is not a data model concern.

The rationale for clustering employee and department data is to improve the performance of joining department records to employee records. In terms of Indemnity Insurance we might similarly cluster holder data with policy data. This would radically improve the performance of common query 1 that we discussed in the previous chapter.

However, clustering must be used with care. The technique is only really

EMPLOYEES

Empno	Ename	Job	Mgr	Hiredate	Salary	Comm	Deptno
7369	Smith	Clerk	7902	17-DEC-80	800		20
20	Research	Bristol					
7499	Allen	Salesman	7698	20-FEB-81	1600	300	30
30	Sales	London					
7521	Ward	Salesman	7698	22-FEB-81	1250	300	30
30	Sales	London					
7566	Jones	Manager	7839	02-APR-81	2975		20
20	Research	Bristol					
7654	Martin	Salesman	7698	28-SEP-81	1250		30
30	Sales	London					
7698	Blake	Manager	7839	01-MAY-81	2850		30
30	Sales	London					
7782	Clarke	Manager	7839	09-JUN-81	2450		10
10	Accounting	London					
7788	Scott	Analyst	7566	09-NOV-81	3000		20
20	Research	Bristol					
7839	King	President		17-NOV-81	5000		10
10	Accounting	London					
7844	Turner	Salesman	7698	08-SEP-81	1500	0	30
30	Sales	London					

etc.

Figure 13.2

effective for stable access paths. In other words, if you know that policy/ holder joins are something you have to do regularly then clustering is a useful option. If you have to do other work with policies or holders then clustering may have a detrimental effect. For instance, ordering holders by their membership of associations is likely to be degraded by the cluster implemented.

In general cluster medium to large tables that are:

(1) Frequently accessed on the basis of some sorted sequence.
(2) Infrequently updated or deleted.

13.3 Adding Indexes

In the last section we considered ways in which we can change the storage of data on disk in various ways to affect performance. In this section we look at a mechanism for improving the access to data without changing the underlying storage structure - the index.

13.3.1 Primary Indexes

The major mechanism for improving performance in relational database systems is the index. Although it is theoretically possible to index on all the data-items in a table, this is rarely done in practice, the major reason being that although indexes can radically improve access performance, they have a negative effect on update performance. In other words, every time we add a record to a table, each index on that table has to be updated. Hence, the more indexes we have on a table, the longer it takes to insert an additional record.

As a bare minimum, we should always index on primary and foreign keys. It is usual to create unique indexes on primary keys. Sometimes this is the only mechanism available for enforcing entity integrity (see Beynon-Davies, 1991b). Since most effective and meaningful joins occur via foreign keys, indexing on these data items can radically improve the performance of such joins.

The effectiveness of indexing can be shown by examining the working of query 1 from our list. Translating this query into an SQL statement would give us something like:

    SELECT claim_no, claim_date, broker_no, product_no
    FROM holders, policies, claims, packages
    WHERE holders.holder_no = policies.holder_no
    AND policies.policy_no = claims.policy_no
    AND policies.policy_no = packages.policy_no
    AND holder_name = &1

(&1 stands for a parameter to be passed to the query).

Suppose that the holders, claims and packages files remain unindexed. All accessing of data in such files will take place using sequential scans. The three joins needed by the query above will be particularly slow.

Now let us suppose we create a unique index on the primary keys *holder_no* and *policy_no*, and create non-unique indexes on the foreign keys *holder_no* and *policy_no*.

    CREATE UNIQUE INDEX policies_p on policies(policy_no)
    CREATE UNIQUE INDEX holders_p on holders(holder_no)
    CREATE UNIQUE INDEX packages_p on packages(policy_no,
    product_no)
    CREATE INDEX policies_s1 on policies(holder_no)
    CREATE INDEX claims_s1 on claims(policy_no)

Note how in terms of packages, since *policy_no* is part of the primary key, an additional index solely on the foreign key policy_no is superfluous. Figure 13.3 illustrates how the logarithmic based retrieval arising from indexing radically improves performance.

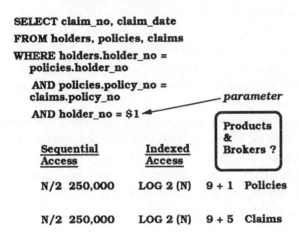

1. Retrieve details of all policies associated with a particular holder, giving details of products, claims and brokers

SELECT claim_no, claim_date

FROM holders, policies, claims

WHERE holders.holder_no = policies.holder_no

   AND policies.policy_no = claims.policy_no   — *parameter*

   AND holder_no = $1

Sequential Access	Indexed Access	Products & Brokers ?	
N/2 250,000	LOG 2 (N)	9 + 1	Policies
N/2 250,000	LOG 2 (N)	9 + 5	Claims

Figure 13.3

13.3.2 Secondary Indexing

We always index on primary and foreign keys. We sometimes index on other non-key attributes of a table, usually when the attribute is extremely important in the running of some report.

In terms of Indemnity Insurance, for instance, we need a facility to list claims by claim type and policies by renewal date. These are two classic candidates for secondary indexing. We build a secondary index on claim_type in the claims file and a secondary index on renewal date in policies.

```
CREATE INDEX claims_s2 ON claims(claim_type)
CREATE INDEX policies_s2 ON policies(renewal_date)
```

In general we build indexes on medium to large tables to facilitate access to a small percentage of rows in a table. We normally build indexes on primary keys. In some RDBMS this is one of the ways of enforcing a column's uniqueness. We also conventionally build indexes to foreign keys to improve the performance of joins. We build further indexes to improve the performance of important queries.

We avoid building indexes if we find that they have a deleterious effect on update performance or take up too much extra space on secondary storage.

13.4 De-Normalisation

The main problem with a fully normalised database is that it is usually made up of many files. To perform useful queries, such files have to be re-constituted via expensive join operations. Also updates frequently have to be performed across more than one file.

One obvious way of improving retrieval or update performance is therefore to step back from a fully normalised database and introduce some controlled redundancy. Control however is the operative word. By re-introducing redundancy we are likely to boost retrieval performance at the expense of reduced integrity maintenance. Below we list some of the most important types of de-normalisation (Rodgers,1989):

(1) Two entities in a one-to-one relationship. In many cases two entities implementing a one-to-one relationship can be combined in one table to reduce the number of join operations. For instance, suppose we have two entities, employee and car, joined by a uses relationship. Even if employee and car are both optional in this one-to-one relationship we may find that only 20% of employees do not use cars and only 1% of cars are not assigned to specific employees. In this case we might be prepared to live with the limited amount of null values in the resulting employee-car table.

(2) Splitting Tables. If there are two distinct transaction types that access different parts of a table, there are possible performance advantages in splitting the table in two. Each table will then occupy less space on secondary storage, less data has to be transferred in accessing a row and more rows can be held in main memory (Howe, 1986).

(3) Multi-Valued Attributes. Multi-valued attributes such as dependents or skills are usually implemented on entity models as separate entities and hence constitute separate files in the resulting database. Sometimes, particularly when the number of such attributes is a

small fixed number, it is more efficient to implement them as distinct columns of the parent entity. In other words we extend the employees table with three columns: dependent 1, dependent 2 and dependent 3.

(4) Reference Data in a one-to-many relationship. Consider the case of the products and business areas files in the Indemnity Insurance database. We see that there are very few records in the areas file. It therefore makes sense to add the area description field to the products file as in figure 13.4. Doing this however means that if for some reason we wish to change the description associated with a particular business area we now have to update multiple records in the products file (Teorey, 1990).

```
CREATE TABLE products(product_no CHAR(6) NOT NULL,
                      area_code CHAR(2) NOT NULL,
                      product_description CHAR(50))
PRIMARY KEY(product_no)

CREATE TABLE areas(area_code CHAR(2) NOT NULL,
                   area_description CHAR(20))
PRIMARY KEY(area_code)
```

```
CREATE TABLE products(product_no CHAR(6) NOT NULL,
                      area_code CHAR(2) NOT NULL,
                      area_description CHAR(20)),
                      product_description CHAR(50))
PRIMARY KEY(product_no)
```

De-Normalisation: OK for files with high access/ low update

Figure 13.4

(5) Derived Attributes. If one attribute is derived from another then in some cases it is more efficient to store both the original value and the derived value in the database. This avoids repetitive computation. The classic example of this is a person's date of birth and age. Age can be derived from data of birth but in many applications age is stored to speed up retrieval.

De-normalisation should only be attempted when all other techniques fail. Try indexing, clustering etc. first before damaging your clean-cut logical design. If you have to, try limiting the damage by de-normalising files with

high retrieval rates but low update rates. In other words choose non-
volatile files. This will limit the amount of problems in data integrity, which
we discuss next.

13.5 Implementing Integrity Constraints

Specifying constraints in design terms for a given application is relatively
straightforward. Implementing constraints however is somewhat more
involved. There are three major ways of implementing integrity constraints:

(1) Inherently. If the data model underlying a DBMS is sufficiently rich
    much work can be accomplished merely using the integrity mecha-
    nisms supported by the data model. In the relational data model, for
    instance, we should at least be able to specify entity, referential and
    domain integrity.
(2) Procedurally. Much of present day implementation of integrity con-
    straints occurs outside the domain of a particular architectural data
    model. Most existing application programs that interface with data-
    bases implement constraints procedurally in third generation lan-
    guages such as C or Cobol.
(3) Non-Procedurally. A third strand of constraint management is however
    beginning to emerge. Many people see the logical place for imple-
    menting integrity constraints as being the data dictionary or system
    catalog associated with the RDBMS (Codd, 1990). Constraints held
    in a central data dictionary offer similar advantages to data held in
    a central database. Constraints would be maintained independent of
    application programs. Data integrity would be enhanced on a corpo-
    rate scale.

In general terms implementing constraints procedurally is far more efficient than implementing constraints, whether inherent or additional,
non-procedurally or declaratively. Just as we have to balance update
performance against access performance, so must we balance update
performance against the need for integrity. We must also judge whether
the benefits of integrity independence outweigh the clear performance
advantages of implementing constraints procedurally.

13.6 Selecting a DBMS

Selecting a DBMS for your application can affect the performance of your application in a number of ways. We examine 3 criteria here:

(1) Coupling.
(2) Compiled vs Interpreted Queries.
(3) Query Optimiser.

13.6.1 Coupling

The DBMS product you choose for your site can have a marked effect on performance. Some DBMS are closely coupled to their operating systems. Because they can exploit directly the access primitives in the underlying operating system they are likely to be better performers than their loosely-coupled cousins.

Loosely coupled systems are designed to be portable across a range of hardware and software platforms. Usually only a very small part of the DBMS is machine-specific.

13.6.2 Compiled Vs Interpreted Queries

Another way in which product selection affects performance is in terms of query-handling. Some systems such as DB2 compile all the queries run on the database and store for re-use the access plans generated. Other systems, such as ORACLE, interpret queries at run-time. As a general rule compiled queries execute faster than interpreted queries. This is because the generation of an access plan need only be done once. However, if your database is volatile or the major form of access is of an ad-hoc nature then interpreted queries are probably more flexible. The overhead involved in compilation of many one-off queries will far outweigh any performance advantage gained.

13.6.3 Query Optimiser

The query optimiser is probably the most important component of a RDBMS. Residing at the heart of the SQL engine, the optimiser is solely responsible for the selection of each query's execution strategy. Relational DBMS need optimisers because of the non-procedural nature of SQL.

There are currently three major methods used in commercially available optimisers for selecting execution strategies (Kellog, 1989):

(1) Assumption-Based Optimisation. This method works on the principle that different operators return different numbers of records. Hence the equals sign - = - generally returns fewer records than the greater than operator- >. Assumption-based optimisers maintain hard-coded assumptions regarding the restrictivity of any given operator. In operation they combine these assumptions with statistics on the number of rows in each table to estimate how many rows will be returned from a table.

(2) Syntax-Based Optimisation. This method assumes that the user will pass optimisation information to the optimiser in the form of the syntax of the query. The ORACLE RDBMS, for instance will show wildly different performance in handling the following two queries:

        SELECT * FROM employees
        WHERE age > 5
        OR salary > 100000

        SELECT * FROM employees
        WHERE salary > 100000
        OR age > 5

The two queries perform differently because the syntax-based optimiser expects in an OR'd list that the most restrictive condition be written first. The first query performs poorly because almost all employees are older than age 5. The second performs well because few employees earn more than £100,000 per annum (Gillaspy, 1989).

(3) Statistically-Based Optimisation. This method allows user-controlled collection of statistical data on the profile of values in columns of tables. The optimiser converts two queries like the ones given above into the same underlying canonical form and then uses the statistical information to determine the number of rows that would be returned by a given restriction. For example, with this information the optimiser can determine that age > 100 is a very restrictive condition while age > 5 is not.

The ordering of the methods above is not meant to imply that one method is always preferable to another. At first glance, for instance, it would appear that statistically-based optimisation is likely to be better than syntax-based optimisation. In some situations, particularly where a lot of ad-hoc querying is being done by end-users on the database, this is true. Syntax-based optimisers however can deliver very good performance when used by a skilled SQL programmer.

The main conclusions to be drawn from this discussion are that, the mechanism having the greatest effect on retrieval performance is the query optimiser, but that every query optimiser works differently. Hence, the same approximate query expressed in SQL may run very quickly on one RDBMS but very slowly on another. Understanding as much as possible about how your particular optimiser works is therefore essential for any good relational physical design.

13.7 Conclusion

We conclude here by suggesting some useful guidelines for good physical design:

(1) Only do physical design after you have conducted a thorough logical design exercise.
(2) State clearly the performance criteria for your particular application.
(3) Be clear as to the balance you must make between update and retrieval performance in terms of your application.
(4) Estimate average and maximum file sizes.
(5) Define the most important access paths and conduct a transaction analysis for your application.
(6) Compute the expected volatility of each of the files in your database
(7) Define the profile of integrity needed by your application.
(8) Consider the use of various storage-related access mechanisms as guided by your volume and usage analysis.
(9) Always index on primary and foreign keys.
(10) Create secondary indexes on common queries.
(11) Cluster on stable access paths.
(12) De-normalise non-volatile files if you must.
(13) Know your DBMS, particularly how the optimiser works.

13.8 Exercises

(1) When is a sequential scan preferrable to indexed access?

(2) Why should we always index on primary and foreign keys?

(3) What is meant by a cluster?

(4) What is meant by de-normalisation?

(5) Discuss the distinction between compiled and interpreted queries.

(6) Discuss the distinction between syntax-based and statistically-based optimisation.

(7) Write SQL queries for each of the common queries 2 to 5 described in section 12.12.

(8) Discuss in each case how you might improve the performance of each query.

(9) Add Cascades, Restricted or Nullifies clauses to the create table statements for Policies and Holders.

(10) Indicate one other area in the Indemnity Insurance database where de-normalisation might be feasible.

Chapter 14
Computer Aided Information Systems Engineering and Database Development

14.1 Introduction

In this chapter we shall discuss the growing number of automated tools for database design. Many people place such tools within the context of CASE - Computer Aided Software Engineering. The author prefers the term CAISE - Computer Aided Information Systems Engineering. CASE may be regarded as a subset of CAISE. Many CAISE tools are involved in the production of software and are hence logically software engineering tools. Many others, particularly those in the database area, are not directly involved in the production of software. Most database design tools, for example, have as their remit the production of structures for storing and manipulating data.

The large number and diversity of CAISE tools makes it impossible to do justice to a representative sample. I have therefore chosen to describe elements of a generic tool-set. Our main aims in discussing this tool-set are:

(1)   To illustrate some of the main features one would expect to see in contemporary commercial products
(2)   To discuss the practical integration of tools to support the entire database development process
(3)   To highlight some of the important advantages arising from the use of CAISE in database development
(4)   To discuss how a number of emerging computing technologies, particularly Artificial Intelligence and Hypermedia, are impacting on CAISE.

14.2 Back-end, Front-end and Integration

CAISE is a logical consequence of a recursive or incestuous view of information systems development. It has stimulated the view that information systems development, considered as an information system in itself, should be subject to and benefit from the same sorts of automation that characterise everyday information systems.

A distinction is normally made between back-end CAISE tools and front-end CAISE tools.

Front-end CAISE tools are generally directed at the analysis and design stages of information systems development. In terms of database development, front-end tools include such products as E-R diagramming editors, determinancy diagramming editors and logical data dictionaries.

Back-end CAISE tools are directed at the implementation, testing and maintenance stages of information systems development. Here tools such as physical data dictionaries, performance monitors and other aids for physical database design are relevant.

Many vendors have now attempted to integrate their front-end and back-end tools. The intention is, for instance, to offer assistance at all the stages of database development, and to expect the outputs from each stage to feed as inputs to subsequent stages. We shall demonstrate in the sections that follow how E-R diagrams, determinancy diagrams, data dictionaries, relational schemas and relational databases are all inherently inter-linked.

14.3 The Advantages of CAISE

Many of the advantages of CAISE arise from automation. Let us examine, for instance, the process of constructing data models in terms of entity-relationship diagrams. It is relatively straightforward to produce small entity models on paper. As soon as we start to scale up the exercise to realistically large levels however many problems emerge. Some paper-based data models end up being displayed at one end of the office and terminate two hundred yards away at the other side of the building! The number of entities, relationships and attributes in such data models makes a paper-based storage mechanism impracticable.

Many of these problems of scale are well-known from software engineering. Much work has been invested in building integrated project support environments (IPSE) designed to support large teams of software developers working on long-term projects. In terms of a large data model we have to ensure that we maintain the integrity of the data model in much the same way as we have to maintain the integrity of an everyday database. We have to ensure that concurrent access to the model is controlled. We have to ensure that the data model remains an accurate reflection of design decisions. We also have to ensure that a history of design decisions are available for inspection.

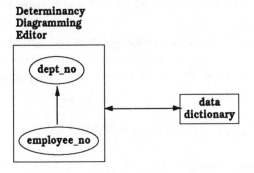

Figure 14.1

14.4 Determinancy Diagramming Editor

One of the tools we would expect to find in our database development environment is a determinancy diagramming editor (see figure 14.1 and 14.2). This tool allows the manipulation of the following graphic objects:

    labelled bubbles - representing data items

    single-headed arrows - representing functional dependencies

    double-headed arrows - representing non-functional dependencies

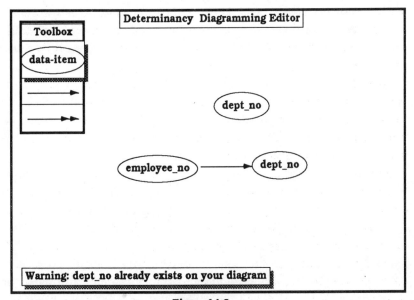

Figure 14.2

Because of the difficulties involved in validating free-form entry of graphics, most of these tools work in a constrained dialogue with the user. For example, the user might select a bubble from the graphics menu. The system then prompts for a data-item name. The user selects a single-headed arrow. The system prompts for a determinant. The user clicks on the bubble he created. The system prompts for the dependent data-item. No such data-item exists. The user therefore selects cancel and proceeds to build a dependent bubble.

14.5 Entity-Relationship Diagramming Editor

An entity-relationship diagramming editor would be a top-down complement to the determinancy diagramming editor (see figure 14.3). Such an editor will manipulate the following graphic objects:

labelled rectangles - representing entities
lines - representing relationships

Crows-feet and optionality circles would be added to a diagram by selecting the end of an existing relationship line and conducting a structured dialogue with the system (see figure 14.4).

At the time of writing, few existing E-R diagramming editors offer all of the extensions discussed in chapter 9. A clustering facility, for instance, would prove an invaluable resource in the construction of large data models. However, the semantics of this technique have not yet been fully formulated.

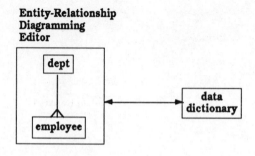

Figure 14.3

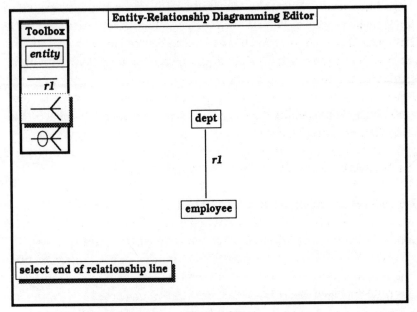

Figure 14.4

14.6 The Data Dictionary

Underlying the activities of the determinancy diagramming editor and the E-R diagramming editor we have a meta-database, which for reasons of consistency we have chosen to call our data dictionary system (see figure 14.5). Here we store all the information about entities, relationships, attributes and dependencies relevant to a particular application.

The data dictionary is the major mechanism for validating the process of reconciliation as discussed in chapter 11. The reconciliation of bottom-

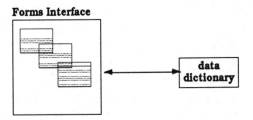

Figure 14.5

up and top-down approaches can occur at a number of different points. Some tools choose to perform all such reconciliation within the data dictionary. Hence, input from the user of the determinancy diagramming editor would be checked off against the results of an E-R diagramming session.

Another approach is to keep the results of top-down and bottom-up analysis entirely separate until an appropriate integration phase.This would mean having to maintain three separate partitions in the dictionary: one for the entity model, one for the dependency model and one for the reconciled model.

14.7 The Accommodation Process

Top-down/bottom-up reconciliation can even be left until the stage at which a relational schema is produced both from our E-R diagram and determinancy diagram independently. As we indicated in chapters 3,4, and 6, well-formed algorithms exist for transforming an E-R diagram and a determinancy diagram into a relational schema. The results from top-down and bottom-up accommodation can then be compared by the system, highlighting any inconsistencies. The system might even prohibit further work until full reconciliation has been achieved.

14.8 Natural Language Interfaces

The editors described above are built for use primarily by professional database designers. In recent years, a number of researchers have attempted to build interfaces more directly relevant to end-users. Most such systems represent so-called natural language interfaces (NLI) to data dictionary systems. The intention is to extend CAISE outward from pure design towards requirements capture.

Using an NLI means entering phrases such as *departments employ employees, an employee has a name and address, salesmen and technicians are employees* directly at the keyboard. The interface interprets each phrase, translates these phrases into entities, relationships, and attributes and writes the information to the data dictionary. The developing meta-base can then be used to conduct a reasoned dialog with the user. The interface might respond with questions such as:

How many employees are there in a department?

Is it possible for a department to have no employees?

Thus the interface will use its accumulated design knowledge to direct its search for further knowledge. Design knowledge comes in two forms:

(1) knowledge specific to the application such as *'employees are identified by an employee number'*.
(2) general design knowledge such as *'entities should have an identifying attribute'*.

The inclusion of general design knowledge into CAISE is fundamentally an exercise in Artificial Intelligence. Much work, for instance, has investigated the application of expert systems to database design.

Figure 14.6 illustrates the interaction of the various interfaces discussed with the meta-base.

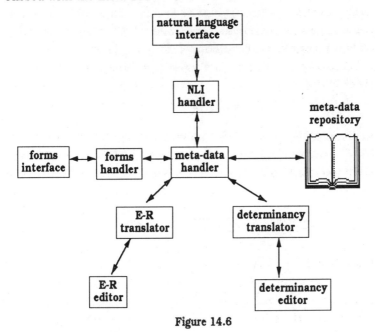

Figure 14.6

14.9 The Design of the Meta-Base

The meta-database at the heart of our CAISE tool for database design is a database in itself. This implies that we should be able to apply the same design principles to the meta-base as we apply to the design of conventional databases. Figures 14.7 and 14.8 illustrate, for instance, how we might draw determinancy diagrams to represent the data needed to

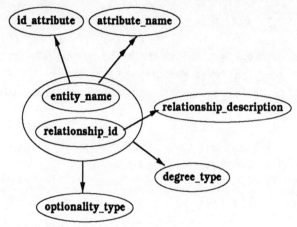

entities(entity_name, id_attribute)

relationships(relationship_id, relationship_description)

entity_attributes(entity_name, attribute_name)

relationship_characteristics(entity_name, relationship_id, degree_type, optionality_type)

Figure 14.7

support the working of our determinancy diagramming and entity-relationship diagramming editors. Figure 14.9 illustrates how information developing for a personnel application would be held in this structure.

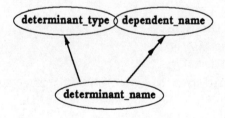

determinants(determinant_name, determinant_type)
dependents(determinant_name,dependent_name)

Figure 14.8

Determinants

determinant name	determinant type
employee_no	functional
department_no	functional

Dependents

determinant name	dependent name
employee_no	department_no
department_no	department_name

Entities

entity name	id attribute
employee	employee_no
department	department_no

Relationships

relationship id	relationship description
r1	employs, is employed by

Relationship_characteristics

entity name	relationship id	optionality type	degree type
employee	r1	mandatory	many
department	r1	optional	one

Entity_attributes

entity name	attribute name
department	department_name

Figure 14.9

14.10 Integrity Constraints

From information held in the meta-base, a back-end CAISE tool should be able to generate appropriate DDL statements in SQL. For example, with suitable data-typing the meta-data in figure 14.9 can be used to produce the following statements:

```
CREATE TABLE employees
(employee_no CHAR(8),
department_no VHAR(8))
PRIMARY KEY (employee_no)
FOREIGN KEY (department_no IDENTIFIES departments)

CREATE TABLE departments
(department_no CHAR(8),
department_name CHAR(20))
PRIMARY KEY (department_no)
```

Note, however, that we have not been able to generate whether deletion of department_no is cascades, nullifies or restricted. However, the system could certainly prompt the user to define the characteristics of each foreign key in the meta-database.

Additional constraints would probably need to be entered via a forms interface to the data dictionary in a similar manner to that discussed in chapter 8.

14.11 Hypermedia and Database Design

Hypermedia is the style of building systems for information representation and management which is based on the principle of connecting a number of nodes of various media together by a series of associative links. Such systems have become popular due to their potential for aiding in the organisation and manipulation of irregularly structured information.

Standard information systems development life-cycle documentation can generally be cast as irregularly structured information demanding the use of various different media for its representation. Database design documentation is a good case in point. The development of any database system demands the use of a system to manage:

(1) Voice. e.g., recorded interviews.
(2) Text. e.g., interview transcripts.
(3) Graphics. e.g., E-R and determinancy diagrams.
(4) Meta-Data. e.g., data dictionary.
(5) Rules. e.g., integrity constraints.

Some existing work has already investigated the use of hypermedia for the management of on-going software engineering life-cycle documents (Garg and Scacchi, 1987). The resulting systems however are primarily passive in nature. They merely serve as a more flexible organising theme for the documentation.

Ongoing research is investigating the place of active hypermedia systems for database design. The intention is to build hypermedia systems for design work that incorporate some degree of 'intelligence'. This area clearly falls within the boundaries of hypermedia systems and artificial intelligence.

14.12 Conclusion

In this chapter we have discussed the place of computer aided information systems engineering tools in the database development process. We have used one system to illustrate a number of features of contemporary CAISE tools as well as identifying a number of possible directions for the future enhancement of CAISE. Nevertheless, database development is still very much a human-intensive activity. Only humans can determine the meaningful symbols they wish to store on some data manipulation device. It is to this problem of meaning that we now turn.

14.13 Exercises

(1)   What is CAISE?
(2)   Describe the distinction between front-end and back-end CAISE tools.
(3)   What are the advantages of CAISE?
(4)   What is a natural language interface?
(5)   Why is a meta-base at the heart of our CAISE tool?
(6)   What is hypermedia and how is it applicable to database development?
(7)   Amend the determinancy diagram in figure 14.7 to include the generalisation mechanisms described in chapter 9.

Chapter 15
The Sociology and Semiology of Database Design

15.1 Introduction

Recently Backhouse et al (1991) have called for a focus for information systems research. They have proposed an organising framework based on the disciplines of sociology and semiology:

> *Two well-established areas of study provide us with a firm foundation on which to build. These are sociology on the one hand and semiology on the other. The former already constitutes the main thrust of research into social organisation, institutional dynamics, group interaction, working conditions and social policy. The latter brings together the range of studies associated with contexts of language and communication, meanings, grammars, signs and codes.*

The author is very much in sympathy with this proposal (Beynon-Davies,1990). What is clearly needed however is a number of practical demonstrations of the utility of this framework, particularly for information systems professionals.

This chapter discusses a personal attempt to locate this framework within practical information systems work. It constitutes an essay on the way in which a branch of information systems development - database design - takes its context from a sociological and semiological analysis. The two major objectives of this chapter are:

(1) To discuss strategies for teaching this material to undergraduate students of computing.
(2) To identify potential new directions of research in the database area.

We first place database design in a sociological context by providing a critique of the *preferred reading* of database design given in the literature. A discussion follows of a small case study in database design. This study has been presented to Computer Studies undergraduates by the author in an attempt to illustrate the way in which database development is at least as much a sociological exercise as it is a technical exercise.

The second part of the chapter develops a short semiological analysis of entity-relationship diagramming (E-R diagramming). Using the example of the case study we illustrate how the conception of an E-R diagram as a sign system explicates some of the key problems experienced in the teaching of data analysis.

In Beynon-Davies (1989) I discussed the premise that information systems development, as exemplified in the process of developing databases, is primarily a task of *conceptual modelling.*, that is, a process of successive refinement through a number of different levels of information model. Systems analysis is requirements modelling, systems design is logical modelling, and systems implementation is physical modelling.

A database is a model of an evolving real world. The state of a database, at a given instance, represents the knowledge it has acquired from this world. But as Sowa cogently puts it:

> *...models are abstractions of reality. The systems analyst or database administrator must play the role of philosopher-king in determining what knowledge to represent, how to organise and express it and what constraints to impose to keep it a consistent, faithful model of the outside world.* (Sowa, 1984)

15.2 Five Key Assumptions

This model of database development is useful in identifying database design with abstraction. As a model itself however it is overly simplistic. This is because, as an instance of conventional systems development practice, it is founded on a number of key assumptions about the nature of reality (Hirschheim and Klein, 1989):

Objective Reality. Most database design techniques treat the real world as given. They assume that there is one reality that is measurable and the same for everyone.

Objective Management. Management is assumed to lead an organisation via clearly defined system objectives designed to improve organisational efficiency.

Technical Expertise. The primary role of the database developer is to be expert in the technology, tools and methods of database development.

Reality Modelling. Database systems development is the task of designing systems that model reality. Database systems are cast as utilitarian tools for management to achieve their ends.

Organisational Consensus. Polemical issues or organisational 'politics' are irrational and interfere with maximum efficiency and effectiveness. As such, they are treated as external to the realms of consideration.

In essence these assumptions are based on a limited conception of the culture of organisations. Organisations are generally presented in the database literature as well-structured formal systems. The application of information systems occurs within a relatively well-bounded area of this formal domain. Figure 15.1 illustrates this idea.

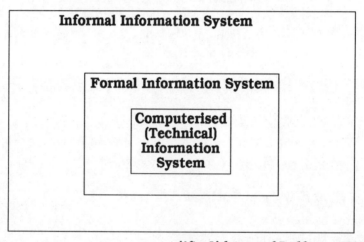

(After Liebenau and Backhouse, 1990)

Figure 15.1

15.3 A Critique of Assumptions

The assumptions described above are clearly open to a critique from a sociological position:

Subjective Reality. Reality is socially constructed. Reality is a continuing negotiation between actors in the social world (Berger and Luckman, 1971).

Subjective Management. Management frequently do not have any clearly defined goals. They may also hold objectives which conflict with organisational effectiveness.

Human Expertise. Most data analysts find themselves doing more human-related work than technical-related work (Beynon-Davies, 1990). Technical expertise is often used more as a vehicle for exercising power over users than as a tool for improving organisational efficiency (Markus and Bjorn-Anderson, 1987).

Reality Shaping. Database design is usually about modelling one particular group's conception of reality. This conception may conflict with the perceptions and expectations of other organisational groups. Information systems development is not simply 'engineering'. It is as least as much organisational innovation (Keen, 1977).

Systems Conflict. Polemical issues are the stuff of which information systems are made. The management (not necessarily the resolution) of polemics is probably one of the best ways of improving organisational efectiveness (Keen and Gerson, 1981).

Any formal information system takes its context or direction from the informal system that surrounds it. The informal information system sets the shape of the organisational reality. It determines the shape of management objectives and determines the direction of organisational politics.

15.4 A Case Study in Design

In the text which follows we detail a short narrative description of the workings of an existing manual system. This is initially presented to computer studies students as a problem in systems analysis. Using the information provided as a starting point they are asked first to conduct a conventional data analysis of the system.

> *Goronwy Galvanising is a small company specialising in treating steel products such as lintels, crash barriers, palisades etc., produced by other manufacturers. Galvanising, in very simple terms, involves dipping steel products into baths of molten zinc to provide a rust-free coating. Untreated steel products are described as being black products. Treated products are referred to as being white products. There is a slight gain in weight as a result of the galvanising process.*
>
> *Black products are delivered to Goronwy on large trailers. Each trailer carries a series of bundled products known as batches. A batch is made up of a number of steel products of the same type*

and is labelled with a unique job number. Each trailer may be loaded with a number of different types of steel product and is labelled with its own advice note detailing all the associated jobs on the trailer.

Goronwy mainly process lintels for a major steel manufacturer, Blackheads. The advice note supplied with trailers of Blackhead's lintels is identified by an advice number specific to this manufacturer. Each job is identified on the advice note by a job number generated by Blackhead's own check-digit routine.

Smaller manufacturers like Pimples supply an advice note on which jobs are identified by a concatenation of the advice number and line number on which the job appears.

Each job, whether it be for Blackheads or Pimples, is also described on the advice note in terms of a product code, a product description, item length, order quantity and batch weight. Each advice is dated.

When Goronwy have treated a series of jobs they will stack white material on trailers ready to be returned to the associated manufacturers. Each trailer must have an associated advice note detailing material on the trailer. Partial despatches may be made from one job. This means that the trailer of white material for despatch need not correspond to the trailer of black material originally supplied to Goronwy. The despatch advice is given a unique advice number and is dated. Each despatch details the job number, product code, description, item length, batch weight, returned quantity and returned weight.

Later on in the discussion the idea of an informal information system is introduced. Concepts such as norms, social roles and organisational sub-cultures are discussed. The key analogy is made between the systems analyst and the social anthropologist. This serves to prepare students for a small exercise in organisational analysis.

The organisation at Goronwy is made more concrete by providing three short sketches of key players in the systems project: Richard Sawyer, Robin Fryer and James Richards. These are meant to represent stereotypes of user-positions. The sketches are presented below.

Richard Sawyer. *Richard is a systems consultant from the headquarters of the owning company. Richard feels his remit is* to quality control critical aspects of the project. The systems consultancy division never code systems themselves. They are expected however to oversee all systems development within the parent company.

Robin Fryer. Robin is the works manager at Goronwy. Robin wants a computer system to enhance the prestige of his brand-new plant. If the system is seen to be successful then it will probably be demanded by other galvanising plants. Robin is also of the impression that a computer system will give him a 'tighter-ship'.

James Richards. James is the production controller at Goronwy. James will eventually be given responsibility for running the information system. He is however less than happy with the project. He feels that the system is unlikely to be worthwhile. He's perfectly happy with the existing manual system.

The exercise in organisational analysis is then portrayed in the following terms:

You are a contractor brought in to develop a micro-based system for production control. Dick and Robin have already discussed the proposed system in depth, and Dick has produced an initial requirements analysis/system specification which he presents to you at the first development group meeting.

Produce, in writing, a brief description of how you think the development will progress. In particular, address the following questions:

(1)   What do you think your role is going to be?
(2)   What role do you think Dick, Robin and James will take?
(3)   Who do you think is the best person to talk to concerning how the system should look?
(4)   What problems do you expect to encounter?
(5)   How do you think the new system will be used?

In two years of running this exercise the author has been pleasantly suprised at the results. Working in groups, most students see the relevance of an analysis of informal systems as part of systems analysis. There is still however something of a social engineering ethos which comes across in the responses. The excerpt below is a composite of some of the best responses I have received from students:

What do you think your role is going to be?

Dick sees me as a lackey. I am going to build a system to his spec. Robin sees me as a miracle-worker. I am going to solve all his problems.

James feels I am going to make his life difficult, perhaps even get him the sack.

My role is actually a 'pig-in-the-middle'. I need to keep everyone as happy as possible, if the system is going to be successful.

What role do you think Dick, Robin and James will take?

Dick is a know-it-all who will want to oversee the project. Robin is not really interested in the specifics of the project. He just wants to see the results.

James is depressed and will do everything in his power to put a spanner in the works, unless I persuade him otherwise.

Who do you think is the best person to talk to concerning how the system should look?

I have to talk to everybody, but James is probably the person I should talk to the most, from day one.

James only knows the specifics of Goronwy. If the intention is to make this system a 'flagship' for other plants then Dick's point of view must also be taken into account.

What problems do you expect to encounter?

Dick being bossy, Robin being confused and James being down-right awkward.

I need to bolster James' enthusiasm. I need to dampen some of Robin's enthusiasm. I need to preserve Dick's position without straight-jacketing myself.

How do you think the new system will be used?

If I upset James it will never be used or he will use it incorrectly.

The objectives of this exercise are summarised in a series of morals presented to students:

(1) *People problems are probably the most important problems in information systems development.*

(2) *Most systems development projects fail because of people problems.*

(3) *Systems maintenance is a people problem.*

(4) *Always investigate people interactions before anything else.*

The overall intent of this exercise is to illustrate the type of material that is needed to redress the technicist imbalance in Computer Studies training. Computer Studies students, in my experience, generally treat the findings of behavioural science with some disdain. This, I feel, is largely because they see no direct practical application of such findings to the problems of information systems development. What is clearly needed therefore is more material which demonstrates the importance of social science concepts to information systems work.

15.5 Semiotics and Semiosis

In this section we turn our attention from a global analysis of sociological context to a specific analysis of the application of semiotics to database design.

Semiotics or semiology is the discipline which studies semiosis. Semiotics is the study of communication and understanding. Semiosis is the process by which communication and understanding occur.

Semiotics is not usually seen as an academic discipline. It is more accurately portrayed as a theoretical approach and its associated methods of analysis (Stamper, 1973). The father of semotics is usually seen to be the Swiss linguist Ferdinand de Saussure. In 1916 he published a work in which he suggested a *science that studies the life of signs in society* (de Saussure, 1916). This suggestion was taken up by the French academic Roland Barthes who is chiefly held to be responsible for popularising semiotics in the 1960s (Barthes, 1973).

Semiotics as a method takes most of its terminology from linguistics. It is not suprising therefore to find that semiotics uses spoken language as its prime example of a sign system. The growth of semiotics however is not so much due to its contribution to the analysis of speech but to its analysis of other sign systems. It has been particularly successful in its analysis of literature, cinema, advertising, photography and television.

Figure 15.2 illustrates the fundamental model of semiosis. A sign stands-for a referent. Hence, a baby crying might be taking as signifying hunger, flags might be taken as signifying nations, flowers might be taken as signifying love. Signs are however inextricably linked with agents. The stands-for relation is inextricably intertwined with human interpretation. Although one person might interpret a given sign as standing for a given referent, another person might disagree. He might take it as signifying something entirely different. Hence, statements about agents, signs and referents cannot be made in isolation from each other (Eco, 1976).

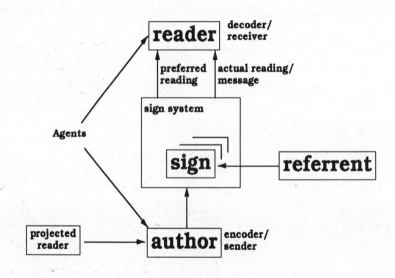

Figure 15.2

The literature also discusses the inter-linked processes of authoring and reading sign-systems (frequently referred to as texts). Sless discusses the way in which, for instance, authoring a text cannot take place without projecting a reader of the text (Sless, 1986). The process of writing this book, for instance, could not take place without some idea of its proposed audience.

A text is open to a number of potential readings, but normally is said to prefer one. Hence, it is usual to refer to the preferred reading of a text. Alternative readings to the preferred one usually derive from differences in the cultural experience of author and reader. Hall et al (1980), for instance, make a useful distinction between three main types of readings. The texts they refer to are actually TV programmes.

(1) The dominant reading which accepts the text according to the assumptions of the encoder. This is the preferred reading.
(2) The negotiated reading which accepts the legitimacy of the dominant assumptions, but adapts the reading to the specific social conditions of the reader.
(3) The oppositional reading which produces a decoding that is radically opposed to the preferred reading.

Liebenau and Backhouse, after Stamper (1985), discuss semiotics as having a four-layered architecture (Liebenau and Backhouse, 1990). Any sign system is seen as having a number of properties:

Pragmatics. The study of the general context and culture of communication. The shared assumptions underlying communication and understanding.
Semantics. The study of the meaning of signs. The association between signs and behaviour.
Syntactics. The logic and grammar of sign systems.
Empirics. The physical characteristics of the medium of communication.

Pragmatics and semantics study the content and purpose of communication. Syntactics and empirics study the forms and means of communication. Pragmatics and semantics clearly impinge upon other disciplines such as sociology and politics. Syntactics and empirics impinge upon the domain of psychology and indeed even electronics.

15.6 Entity Modelling as a Sign System

The earlier quote by Sowa portays database development as building an abstraction of reality. This seems to place Sowa in the camp of those persons who assume that there is an objective reality to be abstracted from. We did however something of an injustice to Sowa in deliberately leaving off a crucial last sentence from the quote:

> *To do a good job in analysing reality, a systems analyst must be*
> *sensitive to semantic issues and have a working knowledge of*
> *conceptual structures.* (Sowa, 1984)

Sowa, from this and other statements in his impressive work, clearly recognises the importance of meaning in the development of database systems. This follows the tradition of portraying probably the most important part of database design - requirements analysis - as *semantic modelling* (Date, 1990).

However, there is something of a sleight-of-hand in the literature on database design. Although the importance of semantics is recognised, the primary area of research in the database area has been devoted to the form of semantics rather than the content of meaning. Much work has gone into proposing architectures for representing semantics - the so-called semantic data models (Peckham and Maryanski, 1988). Little investigation has taken place into the social and psychological process by which meaning is produced. Little effort has been devoted to investigating the way in which, for instance, semantic data models facilitate the capture of meaning. Little work has been directed at viewing semantic data models as tools for shaping conceptions of reality.

15.7 Entity-Relationship Diagramming

Consider probably the most commonly used of all the semantic data models - the entity-relationship model (E-R model) (Chen, 1976).

Klein and Hirscheim (1987) have presented a valuable framework for analysing the philosophical assumptions underlying data modelling techniques such as E-R diagramming. They discuss how current approaches to entity modelling '...follow in the footsteps of an objectivist tradition. Reality is a given, 'out there' and made up of discrete chunks which are called entities. Entities have properties or attributes. Both entities and their properties have an objective existence'. They contrast this with what they refer to as rule-based approaches to data modelling. Such approaches are heavily influenced by the subjectivist tradition. Their proponents see the main task of data modelling as formalising the meaning of messages which are to be exchanged among a professional community'.

The main problem with this dichotomy however is that it assumes that the theory of data modelling is necessarily the same as the practice of data modelling. The theory of data modelling, which unfortunately is the most heavily documented, emphasises the syntactics. The practice, which is poorly documented, is firmly based in semantics.

In other words, the database literature is heavily represented by notations and methods. The actual practice of applying these techniques is heavily resonant with the task of interpreting meaning.

To highlight this distinction we examine in the next section E-R diagramming as a semiotic system.

15.8 A Semiotic System

E-R diagramming is a semiotic system. When we teach a technique such as E-R diagramming we are also attempting to impart something of a method for interpreting reality.

Let us illustrate this idea first by considering a simple example and second by considering the application of this principle to the case study described above.

Suppose you are given the task of drawing an E-R diagram to represent a social convention such as *marriage*. As we mentioned in chapter 7, the common difficulty experienced in drawing such a diagram is to decide whether marriage should be represented as an entity, relationship or attribute. In other words, we must choose to represent the same referent by a selection from a set of three possible signs.

In making such a selection however we are interpreting the world. Each possible sign has a computational significance which must be taken into account in the selection. Entities normally compute as files, relationships compute as integrity constraints and attributes compute as fields. Hence, if we model marriage as marital status (an attribute) we are explicitly assigning it a lesser role in our sign system than if we make it an entity or a relationship.

Semiosis can be seen at work in the process of teaching data analysis. If you set students a simple problem in E-R diagramming like the one described above, the process of interpretation is made problematic. If you set a slightly more involved problem in design it becomes even more problematic. Providing a short snippet of description of some system is insufficient in itself to determine a solution to the problem. Students have to supply background knowledge and make assumptions. Many of these assumptions are based upon the process of projecting a reader for the system. Using the example of marriage again, making marriage *marital status* means projecting an implementation of a project as something like a personnel system. Making marriage an entity however means projecting a system such as a marriage registry.

To consider a more detailed problem, how does semiotics serve to enhance the data analysts' understanding of the Goronwy Galvanising system? Some suggestions are given below:

(1) At the micro-level, three different signs *batch*, *job*, and *order-line* seem at first glance to represent the same referrent - a bundle of steel products to be processed by the plant. However, the projected reader or agent of the sign is different in each case. A batch is a sign used by people unpacking deliveries and bundling despatches. A job is of relevance to people galvanising the material. An order-line is of relevance to clerks recording details of deliveries.

(2) At the system level, four different meanings can be assigned to the proposed production control system. Robin reads it as a status symbol, Jim reads it as a necessary chore, head office reads it as an experiment in information technology.

(3) Authoring any requirements specification for a system therefore involves necessarily taking a position and projecting a readership. If there are a number of readers such as head-office, Robin, Jim etc. then the analysis must involve a heavy amount of negotiation as to the true meaning of the text.

In some senses the process of semiosis would appear to be recognised by the technique of view modelling and view integration. This technique allows for the possibility that an entity model developed in association with a particular user or user-group may be different from entity models produced by other users and groups. Each of these so-called user views is subject to a process of integration. The purpose of this process is to build some form of consensus representation of a database design.

At first glance this technique seems to employ a more subjective assumption of reality than the preferred reading in the database literature. User views however are not usually seen as distinct versions of reality. They are normally portrayed as being different perspectives of the same underlying reality. There is still an assumption that at the end of the integration phase a consensus view of reality can be reached.

One conclusion we may draw from this analysis is that entity modelling is a process of semiosis that occurs in both the formal and informal systems domain. We might even say that the technique is usefully employed at the boundaries of formal and informal systems.

Entity modelling cannot take place without some assumptions taken from the informal context of organisations. An analysis of informal systems is therefore a necessary prerequisite for any data modelling work (Checkland, 1981) (Avison and Wood-Harper, 1990).

15.9 Conclusion

We summarise here some of the conclusions that may be drawn from the discussion above. We place our comments under the two headings of pedagogy and potential research areas.

Pedagogy

(1) A sociological and semiological analysis of database work offers numerous insights into the underlying problems of this activity. Many of these insights revolve around the limited representation or model of systems development employed in the literature. Contemporary systems development practice is founded on a number of key assumptions. Each of these assumptions can be criticised on sociological and semiological grounds.

(2) It is important that students of information systems (particularly computer science and computer studies students) gain an appreciation of the usefulness of such a sociological and semiological analysis.

(3) Such an appreciation cannot be successfully imparted without concrete exercises in the analysis of informal systems.

Research

(1) Database research has primarily devoted attention to an analysis of form rather than content. To use Liebenau and Backhouse's organising framework for semiotics, most database research has fallen into the area of empirics and syntactics. Little attention has been paid to the pragmatic and semantic nature of database work. Hence although semantics has been seen to underpin the database design process, most research has concentrated on suggesting modelling mechanisms

with increased semantic content. Little attempt has been made to address semantics as a process of negotiation between user-groups and database designers.

(2) Two strands of research into the pragmatics and semantics of database work demand further investigation. First, further examples of the application of a semiotic framework to practical projects in database design are needed. Such work is particularly needed to illustrate the process of database design in its guise as a reality-shaping exercise.

(3) Second, a number of research projects are needed to critically examine the technology of database design. For instance, an analysis of semantic data models in terms of sign systems. Do abstraction mechanisms facilitate communication? Which modelling mechanisms encourage negotiation?

15.10 Exercises

(1) Describe some of the key assumptions underlying conventional systems development.
(2) What is semiotics and how is it applicable to database development?
(3) Draw an entity-relationship diagram for the case of Goronwy Galvanising.
(4) Draw a determinancy diagram for the Goronwy application.
(5) Produce a relational schema from your E-R and determinancy diagram.

Appendix 1

In this appendix we provide a number of short case studies that can be used as exercises in database design. Most of the case studies are open-ended. They can be used as exercises in determinancy diagramming and/or entity-relationship diagramming. With a little thought, these exercises can also be used as experiences in physical design. Sample solutions can be obtained from the author.

A1.1 Industrial Placement

Most British Polytechnics offer four year sandwich degrees. A sandwich degree is so-called because it sandwiches one year of industrial experience between three years of academic teaching. The industrial placement officer of your local Polytechnic wishes to set up a database to store details of students on their industrial placement year, and students currently undergoing interviews for placement.

The officer currently records the following details about students currently on placement: student's name, sex, address and date of birth, as well as details of the student's current employer. Each student is also given a supervisor for the year. Each supervisor is required to make three trips to the employer during the placement year. Details held of each supervisor are: name, room number and extension.

Details of students currently undergoing interviews for placement are more complex. Currently, letters of application are sent out to employers from students. Each letter is given a unique code and is dated. Each student will make a number of applications of this type. The placement officer must therefore know the result of each letter in terms of whether or not the student has been requested to attend for interview. Each interview of a student by a given employer is given a unique code. The date of the interview is also recorded, as well as the result of the interview (e.g., offer made, no offer made). Students are obliged to accept the first offer given.

A1.2 Car Hire

Easyhire Ltd is a nationwide car hire company. Easyhire maintains two types of organisational unit: depots and hire-points. Depots are places where cars are held and maintained. Hire-points are places where customers hire cars.

Any one hire-point has access to many depots. Each depot may supply cars for many different hire-points.

Customers pick-up cars from depots and return cars to depots. Customers have to pick up cars from a specified depot but may return cars to any depot of their choice.

Employees of Easyhire are categorised as either hire-point or depot employees. Depot employees remain at a particular depot. Hire-point employees however frequently move between hire-points although each hire-point employee has a fixed group of hire-points at which he or she may be resident.

The requirement is to build a database system that keeps track of where cars are being held, where and who has hired them, and the movement of employees.

A1.3 Cinema-Land

Cinema-Land is a company which owns a number of cinemas in the UK. They require a corporate database to be produced recording details of cinemas, venues, and takings.

Each cinema is given a unique code. Other attributes include the cinema's name, its seating capacity, the number of employees, its location and its manager. Cinemas show a number of films over a season. The company needs to know what films are currently being shown at which cinemas, and what films have been shown at these cinemas.

A venue is a showing of a given film at a given cinema. Venues have a given start date and end date. The company wishes to record the entire takings for each venue and the total number of people attending each venue.

A1.4 Infant Immunisation

A system is required to record details of infant immunisation in a health region.

Every infant in the region is required to have a course of general vaccinations against diseases such as whooping cough and diptheria. Patients are identified by a unique NHS number. Other attributes are his or her name, date of birth, and the NHS number of the mother.

Each vaccination is of a single vaccination type such as mumps, rubella etc. and is given to a single infant. Every infant will however be given a number of booster injections of certain vaccination types at periodic intervals. Each vaccination is therefore given a unique vaccination number. The date of a given vaccination must also be recorded.

Vaccinations are given by general practitioners. A general practice usually has many doctors. Each doctor works for only one practice and is likely to have many infant patients on his list. Each infant patient is on the list of only one doctor. Practices are identified by practice names and doctors are identified by doctor number. The name of doctors and the number of patients on a doctor's list should also be recorded.

A1.5 Telephone Subscription

A telephone subscriber may have one or more installations at his or her place of subscription. Each subscriber is identified by a unique subscriber number. The name and address of the subscriber is also recorded as well as the number of installations. The date of last payment should be recorded against each subscriber.

Associated with each installation there is usually at least one, and possibly several handsets supplied by the telephone company. A handset is identified by a unique serial number. Other attributes are colour and type. An increasing number of handsets are now provided by subscribers themselves. In this case the details are not recorded.

A1.6 A Squash Ladder

You are required to build a small database system to record details for a squash ladder. The ladder is divided into a number of divisions. Each division has a number of positions.

Each squash game has two players and one result. A result is made up of two scores, one for each participating player.

A player can play many games but only with players in the same division. A player can occupy only one position in the squash ladder at any one time. Players are ranked in positions in order of their total scores.

The system should also record the name, address, telephone number and age of each player.

A1.7 Quality Estate Agencies

Quality Estate Agencies is a large company of estate agents. The company wishes to build a centralised database facility for all its branches.

The company's business largely involves arranging sales of residential properties between vendors and purchasers. Details of the property to be sold are recorded from vendors: address, property_type, no_of_bedrooms, garage, garden, asking_price. Each property is given a unique reference number. Details of the vendor are also taken: name, home_telephone and work_telephone.

Purchasers make appointments to view properties. Details of the purchaser recorded includes name, address and tel_no. Details of the appointment include the property number, the date and time of appointment. A given purchaser may make a number of appointments, sometimes to see the same property. Purchasers may also be vendors.

Glossary

Abstraction
The process of modelling 'real-world' concepts in a computational medium.

Accommodation
The process of producing a relational schema from a dependency diagram or entity-relationship diagram.

Active Data Dictionary
An inherent, internal part of a database system, designed to buffer users and application programs from base tables.

Additional Integrity
Business rules of some enterprise. A business rule such as when a foreign key can be null or not in a table.
see Referential Integrity

Aggregation
An abstraction mechanism. The process by which a higher-level object is used to group together a number of lower-level objects.

Association
An abstraction mechanism. Instances of one object are linked with instances of some other object.

Attribute
A column in a relation. A property of an entity.

Bottom-Up Data Analysis
The process of arriving at a relational schema via normalisation.

Bracketing Notation
An implementation-independent mechanism for recording details of a relational schema.

CAISE
Computer Aided/Assisted Information Systems Engineering. Tools devoted to automating various stages of information systems development.

Cardinality
The number of columns or attributes in a relation. The number of instances of an entity associated with some other entity - one or many.

Chasm Trap
A connection trap. A misconception that the relationship between two entities can be generated by other relationships in a data model.

Clustering
The process of storing logically related records close together on some secondary storage device.

Column
See Attribute

Composite Usage Map
An annotated entity model including sizing estimates, cardinality and optionality estimates, and transaction statistics.

Conceptual Model
A model of the real world expressed in terms of entities, relationships and attributes.

Connection Trap
Problem caused by misconceptions in entity modelling.
See Fan Trap, Chasm Trap

Data Analysis
The process of producing a database design.
See Bottom-Up Data Analysis, Top-Down Data Analysis

Data Control Language (DCL)
That part of a data model concerned with controlling database use.

Data Definition
The process of applying the data structures of some data model to the demands of some application.

Data Definition Language (DDL)
That part of a data model concerned with defining data structures.

Data Dictionary
A concept either used to represent the system tables of a relational database or a more encompassing representation of the data used by some enterprise.
See Logical Data Dictionary, Physical Data Dictionary, Active Data Dictionary, Passive Data Dictionary.

Data Integrity
The process of specifying the business rules appropriate to some application.

Data Manipulation
The process of manipulating the data structures applicable to some data model.

Data Manipulation Language (DML)
That part of a data model concerned with maintaining data in a database and retrieving information from the database.

Data Model
An architecture for data. Comprises three primary components: data structures, data operators and inherent integrity rules.

Database
A structured pool of organisational data.

Database Administrator (DBA)
Person given the overall responsibility for controlling a particular database system.

Database Design
The process of modelling real-world constructs in a database.

Database Management System (DBMS)
A system which manages all interactions with a database.

Database System
A system composed of a database and database management system.

Degree
The number of rows or tuples in a relation. Also used as a synonym for the cardinality of a relationship in Entity-Relationship Diagramming.

De-Normalisation
The process of stepping back from a fully normalised data-set to previous normal forms.

Dependency
An association between data items. Data item B is said to be dependent on data item A if, whenever a value for data item A appears, one unambiguous value for data item B appears.

Dependency Diagram
See Determinancy Diagram

Dependency Model
A model of the data-items and dependent relationships pertaining to some application.

Dependent Data-Item
A data-item whose values are determined by another data-item.

Determinancy
The opposite of dependency.

Determinancy Diagram
A diagram which documents the determinant or dependent relationships between data items relevant to some application.

Determinant
A data item which determines the values of another data item.

Difference
An operator of the Relational Algebra. A commutative operator which produces from two tables a table of the rows not common to both tables.

Divide
An operator of the Relational Algebra. Divide takes two tables as input and produces one table as output. One of the input tables must be a binary table, i.e., it must have two columns. The other input table must be a unary table, a one column table. The unary table must also be defined on the same domain as one of the columns of the binary table.

Domain
The pool of values that may be assigned to an attribute or column.

Entity
Some aspect of the real world which has an independent existence and can be uniquely identified.

Entity Integrity
An inherent integrity rule of the relational data model. Every table or relation must have a primary key.

Entity Model
A model of entities and relationships pertaining to some application.

Entity-Relationship Diagramming.
A graphic technique for conceptual modelling. Based on the Entity-Relationship Model.

Entity-Relationship Model
A data model proposed by P.P.S. Chen which models data in terms of entities and relationships.

Extension (of a database)
The total set of all data in a database.

Fan Trap
A connection trap. The incorrect assumption that an entity linking two other entities can act in the capacity of a bridge.

Foreign Key
An attribute of a relation which references the primary key of some other relation.

Generalisation
An abstraction mechanism. The process by which a higher-order entity is formed by emphasising the similarities between lower-order entities.

Hashing
The process by which the DBMS converts the data values in specified columns of a table via some algorithm into a set of storage addresses for records.

Homonym
Same label is used to describe dissimilar entities.

Hypermedia
Style of building systems for information presentation and management based on the principle of connecting a series of nodes of various media together.

Index
A file of pointers connecting logical values with physical storage locations.

Information Architecture
A term used to describe a global data model associated with some organisation.

Information Engineering
A term originated in the work of Clive Finkelstein and James Martin to describe a set of inter-related disciplines needed to build a computerised enterprise based on data systems.

Information Resource Management
The discipline of managing data for administrative, strategic and tactical advantage.

Inherent Integrity
The integrity rules built into the data model as architecture. Entity and referential integrity are the inherent integrity rules of the relational data model.

Integrity
Maintaining the logical consistency of a database.

Integrity Constraint
A rule for maintaining integrity.

Intension (of a database)
See schema

Intersection
An operator of the Relational Algebra. Intersection is fundamentally the opposite of union. Whereas union produces the combination of two sets or tables, intersection produces a result table which contains rows common to both input tables.

IRDS
Information Resource Dictionary System. A repository or record of all the information resources used by some organisation.

Join
An operator of the Relational Algebra. The join operator takes two relations as input and produces one relation as output.

Key
That part of a file primarily used to access records.

Knowledge Engineering
The discipline devoted to building knowledge base systems.

Levelling
The process of building a hierarchical set of E-R diagrams.

Logical Data Dictionary
A data dictionary recording entity model and dependency model information. Used to record requirements independently of how these requirements are to be met.

Logical Database Design
The process of building an implementation-independent model of the data requirements of some application.

Logical Model
An implementation-independent model. The relational data model is a logical model.

Logical Modelling
The process of building an implementation-independent model of some application.

Meta-base
The repository at the heart of a CAISE tool for database development.

Natural Language Interface
A restricted English interface to a database system.

Non-Loss Decomposition
The approach to normalisation in which a universal relation is fragmented via a series of projections.

Normal Form
A stage in normalisation.

Normalisation
The process of transforming a data set subject to a whole range of update anomalies into a data set free from such anomalies.

Object
Some real word thing characterised both in terms of its structural and behavioural characteristics.

Object Model
An entity model with behavioural abstraction.

Object-Oriented
The term designated to computing areas using objects.

Optionality
The participation of an entity in a relationship.

Participation
See optionality

Passive Data Dictionary
A system built external to some database system, designed usually for recording design decisions.

Performance
The ability of some system to achieve a satisfactory level of working.

Physical Data Dictionary
A data dictionary recording details of file structures in a relational database.

Physical Database Design
The process of mapping a logical database design into the structures of some DBMS to satisfactory levels of performance.

Physical Model
An implementation-dependent model.

Physical Modelling
The process of building an implementation of some application.

Primary Key
The identifier for each tuple in a relation.

Production Rule
An IF-THEN rule much used in expert systems work.

Project
An operator of the Relational Algebra. Produces a subset of the columns of a table.

Query Optimisation
The process of transforming a query expressed in non-procedural terms into a query expressed in procedural terms.

Query Optimiser
The automatic engine available in RDBMS for translating non-procedural queries into procedural ones.

Recursive Relationship
An entity related to itself.

Referential Integrity
An inherent integrity constraint of the Relational Data Model. A foreign key value must either be null or a value of the primary key of a related table.

Relation
The fundamental data structure of the Relational Data Model. A disciplined table.

Relational Algebra
The manipulative part of the Relational Data Model.

Relational Data Model
A data model originally created by E.F.Codd.

Relationship
An association between two entities.

Role
The behaviour of an entity in a relationship.

Row
See Tuple.

Schema
A representation of the structure of some database. The intension of a database.

Select
An operator of the Relational Algebra. Produces a subset of the rows of a table. Also the information retrieval command of SQL.

Semantic Data Model (SDM)
A data model having a richer set of constructs for modelling the real world than the Relational Data Model.

Semiotics
The discipline devoted to the study of signs.

SEQUEL
See Structured Query Language (SQL)

Sequential Scan
The form of access in which records are read sequentially from a table.

Sign System
An organised set of signs.

Structured Query Language (SQL)
A database sub-language emerging as the standard interface to relational systems.

Sub-query
An embedded query within an SQL select statement.

Synonym
Different labels used to describe the same underlying real-world entity.

Synthesis
The approach to normalisation associated with mapping dependencies between data-items and building a relational schema directly from such a map.

Table
See Relation

Ternary Relationship
A relationship in which three entities participate.

Top-Down Data Analysis
The approach to data analysis which builds a relational schema from a conceptual modelling technique such as E-R diagramming.

Transaction
A logical unit of work.

Transaction Analysis
A physical design technique involving the analysis of important transactions.

Trigger
An active integrity constraint causing changes to be made to the state of some database when a given condition is met.

Tuple
A row in a relation.

Union
An operator of the Relational Algebra. Union is an operator which takes two compatible relations as input and produces one relation as output.

Usage Analysis

A physical design technique involving the analysis of the usage of some data model.

See Transaction Analysis

Venn Diagram

A graphic technique for illustrating sets. Useful for illustrating the principles of cardinality and optionality.

View

A virtual table. A window into a database.

View Integration

A lateral approach to data analysis.

View Modelling

The process of building seperate entity models to represent user views of some application.

Volatility

An estimate of the stability of some file.

Volume Analysis

A physical design technique. Estimating maximum and average file sizes.

Suggested Solutions

Chapter 1

(1) A structured pool of organisational data.
(2) Data sharing, integration, integrity, independence and abstraction.
(3) A system which manages all interactions with a database.
(4) An architecture for data. Comprises three primary components: data structures, data operators and inherent integrity rules.
(5) Architectural data model equals a paradigm for organising data. Business data model equals a set of business rules.
(6) Relational data model is a minimal data model. Does not maintain any direct mechanisms for modelling abstraction.
(7) Database design is a process of modelling. Database design is a process of successive refinement through three levels of model: conceptual models, logical models and physical models.
(8) There are three core stages to any database design task: conceptual modeling, logical modelling and physical modelling.
(9) Computer Aided Information Systems Engineering.
(10) Design is a knowledge-intensive activity that begins with an informal set of frequently vague requirements and ends up in a systematically defined formal object.

Chapter 2

(1) Enhance program-data independence; treat data in a disciplined fashion; improve programmer productivity.
(2) Data definition, data integrity, and data manipulation.
(3) A relation is a disciplined table. Obeys rules such as no duplicate rows, must have primary key etc.
(4) A primary key is one or more attributes of a table chosen to uniquely identify the rows of a table. A foreign key is an attribute taken from the same domain as the primary key of another table.
(5) Restrict is a 'horizontal slicer'. It extracts rows from the input relation matching a given condition and passes them to the output relation. Project is a 'vertical slicer'. Join combines two tables together but only for records matching a given condition.

(6) It is a language specifically designed for database work. It is not a fully functional programming language.

(7) SQL select implements most of the relational algebraic operators.

(8) Entity integrity - every table must have a primary key. Referential integrity - foreign key values must be a primary key value of another table or null.

(9) A view is a virtual table.

(10) Because all relational operations are performed via the system catalog.

Chapter 3

(1) The process of producing a database design.

(2) Database development involves conceptual, logical and physical modelling.

(3) Easier to develop, understand, and maintain.

(4) Encourages user commitment; leads to better quality systems.

(5) A term originated in the work of Clive Finkelstein and James Martin to describe a set of inter-related disciplines needed to build a computerised enterprise based on data systems.

(6) Encourages a strategic and tactical role for data systems.

(7) CAISE applies the same principles of automation conventionally applied to information systems to the process of building information systems itself.

(8) Knowledgebase CAISE tools are likely to replace contemporary database CAISE tools.

(9) Top-down data analysis starts with things of interest and progresses down to a relational schema. Bottom-up data analysis starts with an analysis of concrete data sets and progresses upwards to a relational schema.

Chapter 4

(1) The process of transforming a data set subject to a whole range of update anomalies into a data set free from such anomalies.

(2) The approach to normalisation in which a universal relation is fragmented via a series of projections.

(3) A relation composed of all the attributes relevant to a particular application.

(4) A set of relations with no repeating groups.

(5) A set of relations with no part-key dependencies.

(6) A set of relations with no inter-data dependencies.

(7) A set of relations with independent multi-valued dependencies modelled appropriately.

(8) A set of relations with interdependent multi-valued dependencies modelled appropriately.

(9) The process of moving back from a fully normalised database to a weaker normal form.

(10) orders(<u>order no</u>, order_date, customer_no)
order_lines(<u>order no</u>, <u>product no</u>, qty)
customers(<u>customer no</u>, customer_name)
products(<u>product no</u>, product_name, unit_price)

Chapter 5

(1) A determinant is that which does the determining; a dependent is determined.

(2) Functional dependencies exist if there is a one-to-one correspondence between values of data-item A and B. A non-functional dependency exists if there are a delimited set of values for data-item B associated with one value of data-item A.

(3) The process of transforming a determinancy diagram into a relational schema.

(4) First to third normal forms are about functional dependency. Fourth and fifth normal forms are about multi-valued dependency.

(5) A method of writing relational schema.

(6)

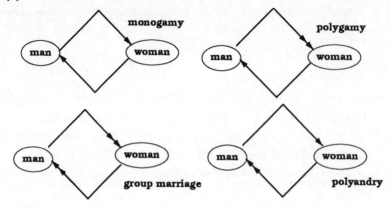

(7)

    (a) marriage(<u>man</u>, woman);

    (b) marriage(<u>woman</u>, man);

    (c) marriage(<u>man</u>, woman);

    (d) marriage(<u>man, woman</u>).

(8)

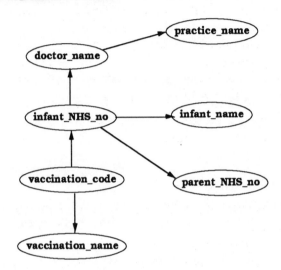

(9) Annotation is not necessary as all foreign keys are part of compound primary keys. In this case, they cannot be null.

Bodies(<u>model</u>, <u>style</u>, market)

Markets(<u>market</u>, main_competitor)

Cars(<u>model</u>, <u>style</u>, <u>engine</u>, price)

Engines(<u>engine</u>, capacity)

Performance(<u>model</u>, <u>engine</u>, max_speed)

Chapter 6

(1) A model of some aspect of the real world expressed in terms of entities and relationships.

(2) Some aspect of the real world which has an independent existence and can be uniquely identified.

(3) Some association between entities.

(4) A property of an entity.

(5) Three: 1:1, 1:M or M:N.

(6) The involvement of entities in a particular relationship.

(7) They help to illustrate instances of entities and relationships.
(8)

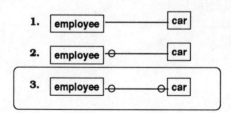

(9) A holder can hold many different policies. A policy can be held by at most one holder. A holder must have at least one policy. A policy must have a holder.

Chapter 7

(1) As circles linked to entities.
(2) Entity identifiers determine all other attributes of an entity. A one-to-many relationship documents a functional dependency between entity IDs.
(3) Makes it easier to accommodate to a relational schema.
(4) courses(<u>course id</u>, course_date, ...)
   attendees(<u>attendee id</u>, ...)
   attendance(<u>attendee id</u>, <u>course id</u>, ...)
(5)

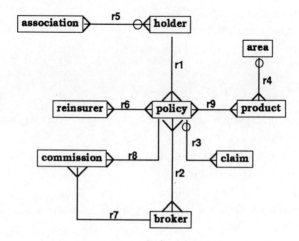

(6) Erroneous reading of the semantics of particular en'

(7)

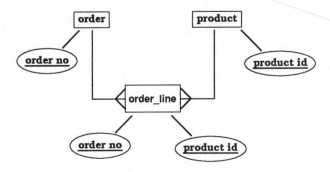

(8) Usually by making relationships many-to-many.

(9) (a) no (b) no.

Chapter 8

(1) A repository for meta-data.

(2) A logical data dictionary records design decisions. A physical data dictionary records implementation decisions.

(3) Passive data dictionaries merely record analysis or implementation details. Active data dictionaries are used to control working systems.

(4) More computationally tractable.

(5)

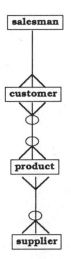

(6)

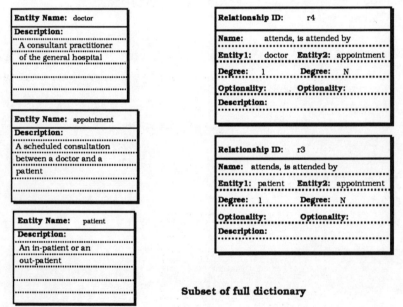

(7) Inherent integrity constraints are built into a data model. Additional constraints are those which cannot be specified in a given data model.

(8)

    (a) inherent;

    (b) inherent;

    (c) inherent;

    (d) inherent;

    (e) additional.

(9) Difficult to document the complexity of many constraints as diagrams.

(10)

Entity Name: doctor
Description:
A consultant practitioner
of the general hospital

Entity Name: appointment
Description:
A scheduled consultation
between a doctor and a
patient

Entity Name: patient
Description:
An in-patient or an
out-patient

Relationship ID: r4	
Name: attends, is attended by	
Entity1: doctor	**Entity2:** appointment
Degree: 1	**Degree:** N
Optionality:	**Optionality:**
Description:	

Relationship ID: r3	
Name: attends, is attended by	
Entity1: patient	**Entity2:** appointment
Degree: 1	**Degree:** N
Optionality:	**Optionality:**
Description:	

Subset of full dictionary

Chapter 9

(1) A relationship of an entity to itself.

(2) A relationship between three entities. Needed for some situations involving fifth normal form.

(3) An entity can play more than one role in relationships with other entities.

(4) 9.1a optional, optional; 9.1b optional, optional; 9.2 optional, op-

tional.

(5) Allow richer conceptual modelling.

(6) Views can implement a version of inheritance by joining tables comprising supersets and subsets.

(7) Representing diagrams as an organised hierarchy.

(8) Object models are entity models with behavioural abstraction.

(9)

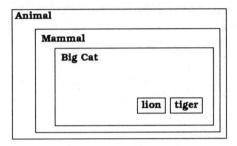

Chapter 10

(1) View modelling is the process of documenting different perspectives. View integration is the process of deriving a consensus schema from these differing perspectives.

(2) Allows for multiple users and multiple developers.

(3) Synonyms, homonyms, mixed constructs.

(4) Allows integration of two entities in a superclass.

(5) To establish a plan for conducting integration.

Chapter 11

(1)

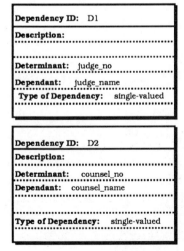

Subset of the Dictionary

(2)

Judges(<u>judge no</u>, judge_name, ...)
Cases(<u>case no</u>, [judge_no], [counsel_no], court, start_date, duration, ...)
Counsel(<u>counsel no</u>, counsel_name, ...)
Offences(<u>offence no</u>, [case_no], [defendant_no], [crime_no], ...)
Defendants(<u>defendant no</u>, defendant_name, ...)
Defence(<u>defendant no, counsel no</u>, ...)
Crimes(<u>crime no</u>, description, max_penalty, ...)

(3)

   (a) Produce a judges schedule for the year ahead.
   (b) Produce a prosecuting counsel's schedule categorised in terms of offences to be prosecuted.
   (c) Produce a schedule of cases categorised by crown courts.

Chapter 12

(1) The process of transforming a logical model into a physical model.
(2) Logical model, constraints, volumes, transaction analyses.
(3) Files, indexes, clusters, constraints.
(4) Update performance is about how fast insertion, deletion and amendment activities take place. Retrieval performance is about how fast we can get a response to a particular query.
(5)

Filename	Max	Avg
judges	100	50
cases	10000	6000
counsel	1000	500
offences	100000	700000
defendants	50000	30000
defence	100000	60000
crimes	1000	700

(6)

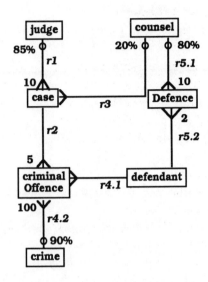

(7)

    (a) Produce a judges schedule for the year ahead.

    (b) Produce a prosecuting counsel's schedule categorised in terms of offences to be prosecuted.

    (c) Produce a schedule of cases categorised by crown courts.

(8)

Transaction Name: Produce Judges Schedule
Transaction Volume:
Average: 2/Day   **Peak:** 10/Day
Transaction Map:

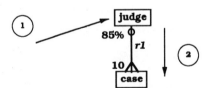

Step	Name	Type of Access	No of References Per Transaction	Per Period
1	Entr_Judge	R	1	10
2	Locate_Case	R	10	100
Total References			11	110

Figure 12.5

(9)

Filename	Volatility
judges	1%
cases	80%
counsel	5%
offences	80%
defendants	85%
defence	80%
crimes	5%

(10) Easier to analyse output from a file than input into a file.
(11) For example:
   (a) Don't delete a judge's or prosecuting counsel's record until all associated case records have been deleted.
   (b) Don't issue a start date for a case until judge, prosecuting counsel and court details have been filled in.

Chapter 13

(1) When more than 20% of records in a file are accessed.
(2) To speed up joins.
(3) Physically locating related information close together on disk.
(4) Sacrificing some of the benefits of a clean-cut logical design for better performance.
(5) Queries are compiled to generate access plans. Interpreted queries generate access plans each time the query is run.
(6) Syntax-based optimisation optimises on the basis of the syntax of a particular query. Statistically-based optimisation optimises from a generated canonical form.
(7)
   (a) SELECT association_no, holder_no, holder_name
      FROM holders, membership
      WHERE holders.holder_no = membership.holder_no
   (b) SELECT policies.policy_no, holder_no, claim_no
      FROM brokerage, policies, claims
      WHERE brokerage.policy_no = policies.policy_no
      AND policies.policy_no = claims.policy_no
      AND broker_no = &1

    (c) SELECT policy_no, reinsurer_no
        FROM reinsurance
        WHERE reinsurer_no = &1
    (d) SELECT claim_no, claim_type
        FROM claims
        GROUP BY claim_type

(8)

    (a) De-normalise by placing association_nos in relevant holder records.
    (b) Possible clustering.
    (c) Clustering index on reinsurer_no or hashed file.
    (d) Clustering index on claim_type.

(9) CREATE TABLE policies(policy_no CHAR(8) NOT NULL,
                            holder_no CHAR(8) NOT NULL,
                            renewal_date DATE NOT NULL,
                            start_yr DATE NOT NULL,
                            premium NUMBER(7,2))

PRIMARY KEY(policy_no)
FOREIGN KEY(holder_no IDENTIFIES holders,
DELETE OF holder_no RESTRICTED,
UPDATE OF holder_no CASCADES)

CREATE TABLE holders(holder_no CHAR(8) NOT NULL,
                         holder_name CHAR(20) NOT NULL,
                         holder_address CHAR(50) ,
                         holder_tel_no CHAR(10))
PRIMARY KEY(holder_no)

(10) Remove membership file as in 8a above.

Chapter 14

(1) Computer Aided Information Systems Engineering.

(2) Front-end tools are analysis and design tools. Back-end tools are implementation tools.

(3) Better productivity; better quality systems; more maintainable systems.

(4) A restricted English-like interface to a database.

(5) To record design decisions in a uniform format.

(6) A style of building information systems that are loosely structured.

Database design documentation tends to be loosely structured in nature.

(7)

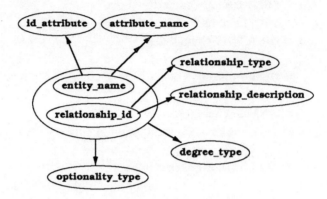

relationship_type = [ako, assoc, aggregate]

Chapter 15

(1) Objective reality, objective management, technical analysts.
(2) The science of signs. Database development is heavily resonant with the interpretation of signs.
(3)

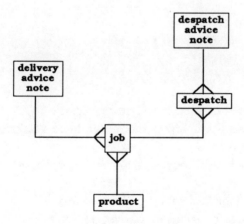

(4)

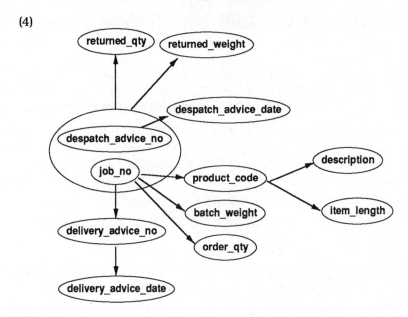

(5)

delivery_advices(<u>delivery advice no</u>, delivery_advice_date)
despatch_advices(<u>despatch advice no</u>, despatch_advice_date)
jobs(<u>job no</u>, delivery_advice_no, product_code, batch_weight, order_qty)
despatches(<u>despatch advice no</u>, <u>job no</u>, returned_qty, returned_weight)

References and Further Reading

ANSI (1986) Database Language SQL. ANSI X3.135-1986.

ANSI (1989) Database Language SQL Addendum 1. ANSI X3.135.1-1989.

Avison D.E. (1991) *Information Systems Development: A Database Approach.* 2nd Edn. Blackwell Scientific Publications, Oxford.

Avison D.E. and Wood-Harper A.T. (1990) *Multiview: an exploration in information systems development.* Blackwell Scientific Publications, Oxford.

Backhouse J., Liebenau J. and Land F. (1991) On the Discipline of Information Systems. *Journal of Information Systems.* 1(1) January 19-27.

Barthes R. (1973) *Mythologies.* Paladin, St Albans.

Batini C., Lenzerini M. and Navathe S.B. (1986) A Comparative Analysis of Methodologies for Database Schema Integration. *ACM Computing Surveys.* 18(4) December 323-364.

Berger P. and Luckman T. (1971) *The Social Construction of Reality.* Penguin, Harmondsworth.

Beynon-Davies P. (1989) *Information Systems Development.* Macmillan, London.

Beynon-Davies P. (1990) The Behaviour of Systems Analysts. *Computer Bulletin.* March.

Beynon-Davies P. (1991a) *Expert Database Systems: a gentle introduction.* Mcgraw-Hill, Maidenhead.

Beynon-Davies P. (1991b) *Relational Database Systems: a pragmatic approach.* Blackwell Scientific Publications, Oxford.

Blaha M.R, Premerlani W.J, Runbaugh J.E. (1988). Relational Database Design using an Object-Oriented Methodology. *CACM.* 31(4) April.

Brodie M.L. (1984) *On the Development of Data Models.* In Brodie et al (1984).

Brodie M.L, Mylopoulos J. and Schmidt T.W. (eds) (1984) *On Conceptual Modelling: Perspectives from Artificial Intelligence, Databases and Programming Languages.* Springer-Verlag, Berlin.

Checkland P.B. (1981) *Systems Thinking, Systems Practice.* John Wiley, Chichester.

Chen P.P.S. (1976) The Entity-Relationship Model: toward a unified view of data. *ACM Trans. on Database Systems.* 1(1) 9-36.

Coad F. and Yourdon E. (1990) *Object-Oriented Analysis.* Prentice-Hall, Englewood-Cliffs, N.J.

Codd E.F. (1970) A Relational Model for Large Shared Data Banks. *CACM.* 13(6) 377-387.

Codd E.F. (1974) Recent Investigations into Relational Database Systems. *Proc. IFIP Congress.*

Codd E.F. (1982) Relational Database: A Practical Foundation for Productivity. *CACM.* 25(2).

Codd E.F. (1985) *Is Your Relational Database Management System Really Relational? An Evaluation Scheme.* Keynote speech presented at ORACLE user's conference. August.

Codd E.F. (1990) *The Relational Model for Database Management: Version 2.* Addison-Wesley, Reading, Mass.

Date C.J. (1990) *An Introduction to Database Systems. Vol. 1.* 5th ed. Addison-Wesley, Reading, Mass.

De-Bono E. (1971) *The Mechanism of Mind.* Penguin, Harmondsworth.

Dutka A.F. and Hanson H.H. (1989) *Fundamentals of Data Normalisation.* Addison-Wesley, Reading, Mass.

Earl M.J. (1989) *Management Strategies for Information Technology.* Prentice-Hall, Hemel Hempstead.

Eco U. (1976) *A Theory of Semiotics.* Indiana University Press.

Fagin R. (1977) Multivalued Dependencies and a New Normal Form for Relational Databases. *ACM Trans. Database Sys.* 2(1).

Fagin R. (1979) Normal Forms and Relational Database Operators. *ACM SIGMOD Int. Symposium on Management of Data.* 153-160.

Fleming C. C. and Von Halle B. (1989) *Handbook of Relational Database Design.* Addison-Wesley, Reading, Mass.

Garg P.K. and Scacchi W.A. (1987) A Hypertext System to Manage Software Life-Cycle Documents. *In Proc. 21st Hawaii Int. Conf. on Systems Science.* Jan.

Gillaspy J.L. (1989) ORACLE SQL Query Strategies. *Database Programming and Design.* March. 50-53.

Gillenson M. L. (1987) The Duality of Database Structures and Design Techniques. *CACM.* 30(12).

Guiraud P. (1975) *Semiology.* Routledge and Kegan Paul, London.

Hall S., Hobson D., Lowe D., and Willis P. (Eds). (1980) *Culture, Media, Language.* Hutchinson, London.

Harel D. (1986) On Visual Formalisms. *CACM*. 31(5) May 514-529.

Hirschheim R.A and Klein H.K. (1989). Four Paradigms of Information Systems Development. *CACM*. 32(10) October 1199-1216.

Howe D.R. (1986) *Data Analysis for Database Design.* (2nd edn.). Edward Arnold, London.

Keen P.G.W and Gerson E.M (1977). The Politics of Software Systems Design. *Datamation.* November.

Keen P.G.W. (1981) Information Systems and Organisational Change. *CACM*. 24(1). January 24-33.

Kellog D.A. (1989) Optimising Queries. *Computer Systems Europe*. May.

Kent W. (1983) A Simple Guide to Five Normal Forms in Relational Database Theory. *CACM*. 26(2).

Klein H.K and Hirschleim R.A. (1987) A Comparative Framework of Data Modelling Paradigms and Approaches. *The Computer Journal*. 30(1) 8-14.

Liebenau J and Backhouse J. (1990) *Understanding Information: an introduction.* Macmillan, London.

Lowry M. and Duran R.K. (1989) *Knowledge-Based Software Engineering. Handbook of AI. Vol 4*. Addison-Wesley, Reading, Mass.

Markus M.L and Bjorn-Anderson N. (1987) Power Over Users: its exercise by system professionals. *CACM*. 30(6) June 498 - 504.

Martin J. (1983) *Managing the Database Environment.* Prentice Hall, Englewood Cliffs, N.J.

Martin J. (1984) *An Information Systems Manifesto.* Prentice-Hall, Englewood-Cliffs, N.J.

Martin J. and McClure C. (1985) *Diagramming Techniques for Analysts and Programmers.* Prentice-Hall, Englewood Cliffs, N.J.

Mcleod D. and King R. (1985) *Semantic Data Models*. In Bing Yao S. (ed.). Principles of Database Design. Vol 1: Logical Organisations. Prentice-Hall, Englewood Cliffs. N.J.

Navathe S., Elmasri R., and Larson J. (1986) Integrating User Views in Database Design. *IEEE Computer* January.

O'Sullivan T., Hartley J., Saunders D., and Fiske J. (1988) *Key Concepts in Communication.* Routledge, London.

Peckham J. and Maryanski F. (1988). Semantic Data Models. *ACM Computing Surveys*. 20(3). 153-189.

Rodgers U. (1989) Denormalisation: Why, What and How? *Database Programming and Design.* December.

de Saussure F. (1916) *Course in General Linguistics*. Fontana, London.

Sless D. (1986) *In Search of Semiotics.* Croom Helm, Oxford.

Smith H. C. (1985) Database Design: Composing Fully Normalised Tables from a Rigorous Dependency Diagram. *CACM.* 28(8).

Smith J.M. and Smith D.C.P. (1977) Database Abstractions: Aggregation and Generalisation. *ACM Trans. Database Sys.* 2(2) 105-133.

Sowa J.F. (1984) *Conceptual Structures: information processing in mind and machine.* Addison-Wesley, Reading, Mass.

Stamper R.K. (1973) *Information in Business and Administrative Systems.* Batsford, London.

Stamper R.K. (1985) Towards a Theory of Information: mystical fluid or a subject for scientific enquiry? *Computer Journal.* 28(3).

Storey V.C. and Goldstein R.C. (1988) A Methodology for Creating User Views in Database Design. *ACM Trans. Database Sys.* 13(3) 305-338.

Sweet F. (1985) A 14 part series on process-driven database design. *Datamation.*

Teorey T.J. (1990) *Database Modelling and Design: the E-R Approach.* Morgan Kaufmann, San Mateo, California.

Teorey T.J. Yang D., and Fry J.P. (1986). A Logical Design Methodology for Relational Databases Using the Extended Entity-Relationship Model. *ACM Computing Surveys.* 18 197-222.

Tsitchizris D. and Lochovsky F. (1982) *Data Models.* Prentice-Hall, Englewood Cliffs, NJ.

Ullman J.D. (1988) *Principles of Database and Knowledge-Base Systems. (Vol 1).* Computer Science Press, Rockville, Md.

Ullman J.D. (1989) *Principles of Database and Knowledge-Base Systems.*

Index

• NOTICE •

Medicine is an ever-changing science. As new research and clinical experience broaden our knowledge, changes in treatment and drug therapy are required. The authors and the publisher of this work have checked with sources believed to be reliable in their efforts to provide information that is complete and generally in accord with the standards accepted at the time of publication. However, in view of the possibility of human error or changes in medical sciences, neither the editors nor the publisher nor any other party who has been involved in the preparation or publication of this work warrants that the information contained herein is in every respect accurate or complete, and they are not responsible for any errors or omissions or for the results obtained from use of such information. Readers are encouraged to confirm the information contained herein with other sources. For example and in particular, readers are advised to check the product information sheet included in the package of each drug they plan to administer to be certain that the information contained in this book is accurate and that changes have not been made in the recommended dose or in the contraindications for administration. This recommendation is of particular importance in connection with new or infrequently used drugs.